HAWAI'I
*Cooks*

# A Korean
# KITCHEN

Star ★ Advertiser

HAWAI'I Cooks

# A Korean KITCHEN

## Traditional Recipes with an Island Twist

JOAN NAMKOONG

Photography by
Ian Gillespie

Mutual Publishing

Library of Congress Control Number: 2013944388

ISBN: 978-1939487-10-0

First Printing, October 2013

Mutual Publishing, LLC
1215 Center Street, Suite 210
Honolulu, Hawai'i 96816
Ph: 808-732-1709 / Fax: 808-734-4094
email: info@mutualpublishing.com
www.mutualpublishing.com

Printed in Korea

All photography © Ian Gillespie, unless otherwise noted below.
Art direction by Jane Gillespie
Cover design by Jane Gillespie
Design by Courtney Tomasu
Photography © Joan Namkoong: pg. 13, 142
Photographs from Dreamstime.com:
pg. iv © Tratong, pg. v © Igor Golovnic
pg. vi (roof tiles) © James Davidson, pg
vi (paper) © Natthawut Punyosaeng, pg
x (top) © Aviavladim, pg. x (paper) ©
Gl0ck33, pg. 9 © Charcharist Dararuan
pg. 12 © Joesayhello, pg. 15 © Jinyoung
Lee, pg. 20 © Natalia Van Doninck, pg.
24 © Linqong, pg. 25 © Matthew Rage
pg. 26 © Photoeuphoria, pg. 31 © Ron
Dayo, pg. 35 © Juan Moyano, pg. 36 ©
Richard Lindie, pg. 38 © Vlntn, pg. 41
Robstark, pg. 47 © Le-thuy Do, pg. 56
Lukas Gojda, pg. 62 © miblue5, pg. 69
Glenn Price, pg. 73 © Robyn Mackenzi
pg. 79 © Marilyn Barbone, pg. 81 ©
Joanne Zh, pg. 82 © Cherkas, pg. 85 ©
Peter Zijlstra, pg. 93, 102 (Korean sushi
© Gregory Johnston, pg. 94 © ouella38
pg. 95 © Elena Elisseeva, pg. 102 (pickl
radish) © Hiroshi Tanaka, pg. 105 ©
Matthew Ragen, pg. 110 © Ivonne
Wierink, pg. 112 © Olga Mark, pg. 115
Gina Smith, pg. 120 © Louella38, pg. 1.
© Barna Tanko, pg. 129 © Bochimsang
pg. 130 © Werner Münzker, pg. 139 (be
peppers) © V.s.anandha Krishna, pg. 13
(bamboo shoots) © Le-thuy Do, pg. 145
© Timhesterphotography, pg. 147 ©
Penglan, pg. 148 © Nilsz, pg. 149 (garli
© Paul Cowan, pg. 150 (pine nuts) ©
Margo555, pg. 150 (radish) © Alian226,
pg. 151 (rice cooker) © Rudy Umans, pg
151 (ttok) © Jinyoung Lee, pg. 152 ©
Ppy2010ha, pg. 153 (soy sauce) © Ippeit
pg. 153 (tofu) © Margouillat
Photographs from iStockPhotography.com:
pg. x (Korean writing) © joxxxxjo, pg.
© kevinjeon00, pg. 50 © miblue5, pg. 5
© miblue5, pg. 63 © SangHyunPaek, pg
86 © JasonArcher, pg. 88 © Creativeye9
pg. 111 © Skystorm, pg. 131 © jkilian,
pg. 143 © marucyan

# Star ✦ Advertiser

*Korean Kitchen* is the first in a series of cookbooks partnering Mutual Publishing and the *Honolulu Star-Advertiser* in an exploration of Hawai'i's many ethnic cuisines. The writers will be a mixed group, united by the fact that they grew up in Hawai'i, learning from their parents and grandparents, aunties and uncles, to prepare the dishes of their heritage, but local-style.

Joan Namkoong is the perfect author to launch our series. A former food editor at the *Honolulu Advertiser*, Joan has long served as an advocate for the home cook and for the food traditions of our islands. As a freelance writer, she has advanced knowledge of the local food scene far beyond these shores. Joan has also championed Hawai'i's farmers and ranchers and played an instrumental role in founding the Hawai'i Farm Bureau farmers markets, which have become weekly institutions at several sites around O'ahu. Joan's commitment to the island food community—from producers to restaurants to home cooks to diners—runs deep. She walks the walk.

At the *Honolulu Star-Advertiser,* we celebrate the diversity of island cuisine every week on our Food pages. We proudly build on that tradition with the series *Hawai'i Cooks* and with this first book, *A Korean Kitchen*.

**Dennis Francis**
President and publisher,
*Honolulu Star-Advertiser* and O'ahu Publications

# Contents

## Chon
### Pan-Fried Foods

## Kogi & Haemul
### Meats & Seafood

## Special Dishes

## Appendix

# Acknowledgments

Writing this book reconnected me with many Koreans in the Hawai'i community. I enjoyed talking with family friends and old timers, learning of their food experiences and comparing them to mine, including Daisy Choy, Agnes Rho Chun, Melvia Kawashima, Robert and June Ko, Joyce Lee, Eldean Scott and Sally Swanhom. Family members Howard Han, Rachel Chinn, Marie Ann Yoo, Elizabeth Backman and Paul Namkoong added to the food memories.

Businessmen Mike Irish and Peter Kim gave their perspective on Korean food in Hawai'i, as did food writer David Choo and chef Kelvin Ro. Jennifer Kim introduced me to new dishes and new foodies; Bill and Yebong Park became my recipe tasters and Joung Nakamoto added her Korean food knowledge.

Special thanks to my cousin Elizabeth Backman who spent many hours at the Hawai'i State Library, going through microfilm and finding precious articles about our family and the early Korean immigrants. And to chef Onjin Kim for the many recipes she provided for this book; she became my foodie resource, explained Korean ingredients and dishes, and expanded my Korean food experience while we traveled in Korea.

To Betty Shimabukuro and Muriel Miura, editors of this series, and Bennett Hymer of Mutual Publishing, thank you for this opportunity to share my Korean food world with others.

# The Hawai'i Cooks Series

This *Hawai'i Cooks* series is not meant to be a guide to the "traditional" cooking of any ethnic group. You can find those cookbooks in any bookstore. These books are a reflection of the various cuisines as they have developed—deliciously—in our islands.

There is a difference. Each immigrant group arrived in the islands over a set period of years, with eating habits that reflected those of the homeland at that time. Back in Asia or Portugal, meanwhile, cuisine grew and changed. This evolution worked both ways. In Hawai'i, cooks adapted traditional dishes to local ingredients. And as circumstances improved, they used more of the sugar and meat that became affordable to them.

End result: Today a visitor from Japan might find our Japanese food recognizable but sweet; a Korean might be surprised by the amount of meat on the typical Korean menu; someone from Portugal might wonder, what is this thing we call Portuguese Bean Soup?

The heritage is to be respected, the differences to be celebrated, the deliciousness simply to be enjoyed.

The *Hawai'i Cooks* series will continue with Portuguese, Okinawan, Japanese, and Chinese cuisines.

## Dig in.

**Betty Shimabukuro and Muriel Miura**
*Editors*

# Introduction

The enticing aroma of soy-garlic-sesame-marinated meat sizzling on a grill at Ala Moana Beach Park is indelible in my memory, as is the taste, hot off the fire, salty-sweet, pungent and oh, so very delicious. Kalbi, Korean barbecued short ribs, is a favorite of mine and a dish few in Hawai'i can resist. Kalbi is among many Korean dishes that have become key to the "local food" repertoire of the multi-ethnic 50th state.

I am a second-generation Korean American, born and raised in Hawai'i, a foodie and food writer who has eaten and cooked Korean dishes for well over a half-century. This cookbook is a family and community history through the lens of food.

My maternal grandparents emigrated from Seoul, Korea, along with thousands who became sugar plantation workers in the early 1900s. My maternal grandfather, Chin Tae Choi, arrived in Hawai'i in 1904 from Chong Dong, Seoul, and served as a Methodist minister to Korean plantation workers on O'ahu, Hawai'i island and Maui. My grandmother, Elizabeth Pahk Choi, arrived in 1912 with my mother, Marie, her twin sister, Salome, both age 8, and brother, Don. My grandfather died the same year, leaving the family to fend for themselves.

My mother was a seamstress, as were her mother and grandmother (my great-grandmother, who was a seamstress in the Yi dynasty royal court). No doubt both learned some of the intricacies of cooking in the palace. In fact, my grandmother orchestrated a Korean banquet in November 1931 for the Korean Women's Committee of the Pan Pacific Union and was recognized as "one of the best cooks in the local Korean community" in a *Honolulu Star-Bulletin* article, November 12, 1931.

My father, Peter Tark Namkoong, came from Hongchun, Kangwando province, in northeast Korea. As a young student from a scholarly family, he won a speech contest that in 1930 took him to Chicago, where he attended Loyola University. My father served in the O.S.S., the forerunner of the C.I.A., during World War II, utilizing his skills in Japanese, Chinese, Korean and English languages. My parents were married in San Francisco in 1943 and set up residence in Hawai'i following World War II.

On July 26, 1952, my father opened Korean Garden restaurant on Ala Moana Boulevard near Keawe Street, one of the earliest Korean restaurants in Hawai'i. The kitchen was supervised by my aunt, Salome Choi Han, with my mother alongside. A menu dated August 1953 shows an assortment of classic Korean dishes—pulkogi, kalbi, chon, mandu, kuksu, namul and of course, kimchi. "Dishes from old Korea with a touch of the Islands" reads the menu, which also included selections for "Haole Food" and "Pake Food."

Few locals had tasted Korean food at that time, but Korean Garden became a place where noted dignitaries and celebrities came to dine. Few Koreans, however, had the means or desire to dine out and transportation was unreliable. Financial and legal difficulties led to the closing of the restaurant.

I remember "playing" in the restaurant as a very young child, sweeping floors and slurping noodles with the cooks in the kitchen. Perhaps the "foodie gene" was passed on during this time.

I helped with kimchi making, frying chon, toasting kim and shaping mandu. My mother prepared special Korean dishes for every new year and would always invite people to partake. I learned to cook these traditional dishes and have entertained many a crowd with these simple, tasty foods.

The evolution of Korean food in the islands has always intrigued me. I have always had the notion that the Korean food I ate growing up is in a time warp, caught in the early 1900s, when my parents came to America. The simple, savory dishes, mostly centered on beef, pork, tofu and vegetables was Korean fare of the early 1900s, adapted in the islands using available ingredients.

Meanwhile, food in Korea evolved, particularly after World War II and the Korean conflict of the 1950s. There were probably periods of limited food resources in Korea, a country that was already lacking in adequate food during the decades of Japanese occupation and the subsequent conflicts. As the country rebuilt and prospered, food resources increased and led to the creation of new dishes as well as the preservation of the traditional dishes.

My repertoire of Korean dishes is very limited in relation to what is being prepared in homes and served in Korean restaurants in Hawai'i today. Part of it, I suspect, is that Korean food was not what we ate all the time; American and other ethnic foods were on the table too, because we were American first, then Korean.

The more recent wave of Korean immigration after the Korean War which escalated in the 1960s and 1970s, brought new ingredients, flavors and cooking ideas that reflect a more affluent homeland with a wider variety of food resources. The establishment of Korean supermarkets and restaurants, particularly in Honolulu, has contributed to the popularity of Korean food in Hawai'i. Along with other local ethnic cuisines, the ingredients and flavor palate of Korean dishes has been incorporated in Hawai'i Regional Cuisine, the defining cuisine of Hawai'i that utilizes locally grown food products in ways that reflect the unique island ethnic cuisines that evolved over time.

This book is about the Korean food I grew up on and learned to cook from my mother and father. It mirrors, I think, the food that many Koreans in the first wave of immigration ate and cooked, utilizing the ingredients that were available in Hawai'i through the years. It is also the Korean food that has become popular among the general population in Hawai'i. But Korean food has evolved, so this book also includes some recipes from the more contemporary repertoire of Korean cuisine.

# Koreans in Hawai'i

Korean merchants arrived in Hawai'i as early as 1899 but it wasn't until 1903 that a major wave of immigrants came to the islands. On December 22, 1902, the S.S. *Gaelic* set sail from Inchon, Korea, arriving in Honolulu on January 13, 1903, carrying 102 passengers.

The 56 men, 21 women and 25 children who made the 22-day voyage left a drought-stricken and politically unstable homeland. Several months before the voyage, Korean King Kojong had lifted emigration restrictions. At the same time the Hawai'i Sugar Planters Association was looking at Korea as a source of labor.

Hawai'i's plantation workers had come mostly from China and Japan. But the 1882 Chinese Exclusion Act blocked further Chinese immigration and labor unrest was growing among Japanese workers. The association, looking for another pool of laborers, posted announcements in port cities in Korea, offering wages that were high to impoverished Koreans, free ocean passage and money to clear customs in Hawai'i.

The first group of immigrants was assigned to Waialua Plantation on O'ahu. Later groups were dispersed to Hawai'i island, Maui and other O'ahu plantations. A 1903 newspaper article described the Korean immigrants as follows:

> The Koreans who came here in January 1903 are a steady lot of men, accustomed to farm work. They begin well, and appear contented and willing.
> The present immigration of Koreans is experimental. If they are found to be good laborers on the plantation and take kindly to the country, there is no question whatever that each steamer from the Orient will see a large company of these people.

During the next two-and-a-half years, 7,843 Korean laborers arrived in Honolulu Harbor in 65 boatloads. The majority were single men. Plantation life was difficult at best and the pay of $16 a month was barely enough to survive on, much less raise a family.

By 1903 Hawai'i was a territory of the U.S., which forbade labor contracts. Most Korean immigrants, no longer bound by their contracts, quickly moved off the plantations.

In April 1905, emigration from Korea was stopped by royal decree. The Japanese government's influence over Korea was growing and it was in the best interest of the Japanese to block the exodus of Korean manpower.

Still, between 1910 and 1924, Korean bachelors were able to send for picture brides from Korea and subsequently the Korean population in Hawai'i stabilized as families increased. Many couples started boarding houses for single men and the women cooked and did their laundry. Others used their skills as tailors and carpenters to earn a living, some started businesses as shopkeepers, peddlers, food manufacturers and restaurateurs.

The early Korean immigrants were different from their Chinese and Japanese counterparts. They came from urban areas all over Korea rather than specific rural farming regions, as was the case with immigrants from China and Japan. They came from all classes of society and many had strong Christian belief systems that equated to familiarity with Western customs, language and foods. These factors and their small numbers, compared to the Chinese and Japanese populations, contributed to a more rapid assimilation into American society.

Most Korean immigrants stayed in Hawai'i. Of the first wave, 1,300 moved to the mainland U.S., most to California, until an executive order in 1907 banned the migration. About 1,100 returned to Korea, versus more than half of the Chinese and Japanese immigrants who returned to their homelands. The Koreans had to "make it" in Hawai'i; the instability of politics in their homeland and the later annexation of Korea by Japan in 1910 left them virtually without an option to return home.

Korean immigrants learned English quickly and had a higher rate of intermarriage than other immigrant workers. They were in Hawai'i to stay and make a new life. Their Christian identity was a factor in their Americanization. Korean Methodist Episcopal Church (Christ United Methodist Church today) was established in 1904; the Korean Christian Church on Liliha Street was dedicated in 1938 and founded by Syngman Rhee, president of Korea from 1948 to 1960;

St. Luke's Episcopal and Wahiawā Christian Church also catered to the Korean population on Oʻahu.

Korea lifted its ban on emigration in 1910 but in the U.S. the Oriental Exclusion Act of 1924 halted further immigration until the end of World War II, when brides of American servicemen and orphans adopted by American families were allowed into the country.

Another wave of arrivals from Korea began in 1965 under the Immigration and Nationality Act that lifted formulas for national origin and allowed immigration based on skills and family relationships with U.S. citizens. Like the earlier immigrants, Koreans were looking for better opportunities; many came seeking better education for themselves and their children.

Korean immigrants have had difficulties applying their skills and education and establishing their lives in Hawaiʻi but they, like other immigrants, have persevered towards their dream for a better life in the U.S.

# About These Recipes

The recipes in this book are based on what I cook and learned to cook from my family. All Korean cooks have their own versions of each dish and their own ways of seasoning. On a visit to Korea, while dining in restaurants and homes, I realized quickly that among the dozens of side dishes I sampled, no two were alike.

Mine is a savory palate rather than a sweet one; I like a balance but don't want sweetness to be the first thing that I notice. Ultimately, taste depends on the cook; there is no right or wrong way with any cuisine. Food is constantly evolving according to the ingredients at hand and the whim of the cook.

The recipes here have been "measured" so you have an idea of quantities of ingredients, although I do not measure when I cook. Feel free to add, subtract or adjust.

Some recipes in this book are from other Korean cooks—those in the community who have shared their knowledge. Frankly, they are for dishes I have little experience in preparing; I have relied on others to fill in the gaps of the Hawai'i Korean repertoire.

Korean meals are all about a variety of panchan, or side dishes, So I have sized many of the recipes to produce a smaller quantity. One zucchini for example, made into chon, will produce about 15 pieces; ample, I think, for four to six people when it's part of a meal of five to seven dishes. Similarly most meat recipes call for a pound of meat; meat has always been a luxury on the Korean table, eaten in small amounts. The concept of an "entrée" is not a consideration when cooking a Korean meal; meats and vegetables play an equal role.

A few notes about ingredients used in testing these recipes:

* Kikkoman soy sauce is an accepted brand in Korea, one with more depth and breadth of flavor than other brands I have worked with. If you find it too salty, Kikkoman can be diluted and I have done this in some recipes.

* Kadoya sesame oil, a dark roasted oil, is flavorful and consistent.

- Korean cooks often use sea salt but I prefer Diamond Crystal kosher salt, even though it may require twice as much as regular table salt to achieve the same result.

- Korean ingredients like kochu jang are available in all supermarkets. Most of us old-time Korean cooks use the Park's brand of kochu jang but I find the Korean ones quite good, too. Look for kochu jang from Sunchang, a town known for its chili pepper paste.

- Most of us still use the Japanese miso that has been available to us all along; Korean toen jang tends to be a bit saltier and more intense in flavor.

- Sweet potato starch noodles are a new discovery in making chopchae. I had been using long rice or mung bean noodles, which have always been on supermarket shelves. Sweet potato starch noodles are chewier and firmer, and I've come to like them very much.

This book is not intended to present a full repertoire of Korean dishes, rather it is a record of dishes that "old-timers"—first immigrants—have cooked in Hawai'i for several generations, as well as some popular dishes cooked by more recent immigrants and served in Korean restaurants today. The distinction is important: The ingredients, seasonings and flavor palate are quite different. Popular Korean food in Hawai'i tends to be bolder in flavor than the food prepared by more recent immigrants; the latter tends to be more delicate and subtle.

Hopefully home cooks will find a good variety of dishes that embody the flavors of a delicious cuisine.

# Ssal
# Rice

**Pap mogo?** *Are you hungry for rice?*

A Korean meal relies on cooked rice, or pap, and everything else is an accompaniment. Sticky, medium- to short-grain white rice is the preference. I grew up eating Calrose (Hinode brand) but today I prefer some of the distinctive Japanese varieties grown in California. Tamaki Gold, Tamanishiki, Akitakomachi, Kohishikari are names I look for. Haiga is another term—rice that is not completely polished, retaining the germ of the grain and more of its nutrition. This type is cooked the same as Calrose; the nice feature is that you can refrigerate it and the grains are soft and moist when cold. Most importantly, these varieties are more delicate, sweeter and just plain delicious.

Koreans often prepare rice with black or red beans, and with grains (millet, barley, sorghum). This began as a matter of economy when white rice was not affordable or widely available, but rice stretched with beans and grains is now considered a nutritious dish.

Before electric rice cookers, we used covered saucepans, bringing the mixture of rice and water to a boil then quickly lowering the heat so the grains could absorb the liquid. It was necessary to keep a watchful eye on the rice pot so the frothy hot liquid would not boil over; nor would you want to neglect the pot until the bottom burned black.

But a golden brown crust of rice at the bottom was desirable. Nurungji, that "burnt" rice, was delectable, as was the sungnyung, or water rice often consumed like a tea at the end of a meal. Sungnyung with salted butterfish always soothed an upset stomach.

Rice is also prominent in Korean confections. Glutinous or sticky sweet rice, aka mochi rice, steamed, then pounded into a paste, becomes ttok, the chewy rice cakes served as a sweet treat or floated in a soup. Round discs of ttok, fried in oil until crisp and eaten with honey, were a childhood favorite. Ttok coated in soybean powder and siru, or layered ttok, again, dipped in honey, were special treats relished at parties.

Like its neighbors, China and Japan, Korea celebrates special occasions with rice, especially rice cakes. Mochi in Japan, gau in China and ttok in Korea are ceremoniously eaten for the New Year, said to usher in good fortune. To this day, I insist that friends joining my New Year's table eat ttok, a sticky, bland slice or two from a log-shaped piece. It does not draw the same praise as the mandu that accompanies it in a bowl of soup.

Another rice treat that my mother often made was yak-pap, also known as yaksik or medicinal food. Glutinous rice is steamed and mixed with chestnuts, red dates, pine nuts, sesame oil, soy sauce and honey into a delightful sweet, sticky confection that begs to be eaten one mouthful after another.

# Pibimpap
# Mixed Up Rice Bowl

When I was a child, pibimpap meant fried rice that incorporated all the leftover pulkogi, chon, namul, egg strips, green onions and whatever else was in the refrigerator from the previous night's feast. Mom stir fried it all together with the leftover rice in a frying pan and served it in a bowl.

Pibimpap—literally, mixed up rice—is a popular dish today: an assortment of vegetables and meat served on a bed of rice, topped with a sunny side up egg and garnished with kochu jang. It is served with flourish, sometimes in a hot stone pot that makes the rice sizzle at the bottom, turning the rice into a brown, crunchy crust.

While some might say this was a dish of the royal palace, pibimpap could have started more humbly like the Korean fried rice I grew up on. Consider that a Korean meal consists of many panchan or side dishes. What to do with all those leftovers after the meal? Arrange them attractively on top of rice, of course, fry up an egg to add a little more protein and serve it with a spicy sauce. The Korean diner, of course, mixes it all up before eating it with a spoon—just like mom did in the frying pan!

Jeonju, in the Jeollabuk province in southwestern Korea, is considered the birthplace of pibimpap, perhaps because it was the birthplace of the Yi or Joseon dynasty. Pibimpap was served as lunch to the king's family when they visited, during the busy harvest season and on New Year's Eve to use up leftovers. It was a dish first mentioned in texts in the late 1800s.

In Jeonju, pibimpap might include pine nuts, walnuts, gingko nuts, jujube (red dates), yellow muk (mung bean jelly); a raw egg yolk is served on top where other places will serve a sunny side up egg. Seasoned chopped raw meat is also an option. Jeonju is renowned for this dish and celebrates it annually with a pibimpap festival within a traditional folk village, showcasing the dish in a variety of traditional and contemporary preparations along with cooking competitions, craft and cultural exhibitions.

Pibimpap is really a meal in a bowl, a nutritious dish of mostly vegetables and a little meat. It can be composed of anything you want—leftovers or ingredients you season just for the occasion. Here's a suggested list of what to put on top of your freshly cooked rice:

**Pulkogi (page 72), cut into strips**
**Korean Barbecue Chicken (page 76), cut into strips**
**Spicy Barbecue Pork (page 74), cut into strips**
**Kimchi Chon (page 62), cut into strips**
**Zucchini or Eggplant Chon (page 53, 51), cut into strips**
**Beansprout or Cucumber Namul (pages 90, 87)**
**Kong Namul (page 90)**
**Egg Garnish (page 106)**

Arrange each item, five or six of them, on top of a bowl of hot rice. Fry an egg, sunny side up, and place it on the top. Serve, accompanied by dollop of kochu jang.

# Ttok Boki
# Spicy Rice Cakes
*Serves 6*

A bubbling pot of red spicy sauce with slim fingers of rice cake is a familiar sight in the street markets of Seoul. It's a tasty and filling snack that's very popular—it's often seen in K-dramas, too. This is definitely a dish of modern Korea and I've relied on Onjin Kim to provide this delicious recipe.

The rice cakes used for this are skinnier than the hind ttok used for soup, about ½-inch in diameter. They are used whole or cut in half. The fish cake used here is a Korean product, thin 5 x 8 inch sheets of tasty golden brown fish cakes. Cut each piece into quarters then cut each quarter into half diagonally to form a triangle.

1½ pounds rice cakes
6 ounces (4 pieces) fish cake
3 tablespoons kochu jang (chili pepper paste)
1 tablespoon kochu karu (chili pepper powder)
1 tablespoon soy sauce
2 tablespoons light corn syrup
1½ teaspoons sugar
3 tablespoons ketchup
1½ teaspoons minced garlic
1 tablespoon sesame oil
3 cups Anchovy Stock (page 156)
½ onion, sliced
½ small head cabbage, cut into 1-inch pieces
2 green onions, thin sliced on an angle
1 teaspoon sesame seeds, roasted and ground

Soak the rice cakes in water for 30 minutes. Drain well.

Cut fish cake into quarters and cut each quarter in half diagonally to form a triangle.

Measure the next 9 ingredients into a large pot and place over medium high heat. Bring to a boil then reduce heat to medium low. Add the rice cakes and onion and simmer for 10 minutes, stirring occasionally to prevent rice cakes from sticking to the bottom of the pan. Add the cabbage and fish cakes and simmer for another 10 minutes. Transfer to a serving dish and garnish with green onion and sesame seeds.

# Ttok Kuk
# Rice Cake Soup
*Serves 4*

Traditional for celebrating the New Year, ttok kuk is like Japanese ozoni, rice cakes in soup. Korean rice cakes are firmer than Japanese mochi; hind ttok is used in soup and it is a smooth, firm, one-inch log of rice. It is sliced on the diagonal into three-eighths inch pieces and boiled in water or broth for a few minutes to soften it. It's not the kind of rice cake you snack on; it must be cooked and eaten hot in a soup or sauce.

Ttok kuk is made with beef or chicken broth and usually garnished with seasoned strips of beef, green onion, egg strips and crumpled seaweed. It is delicious and filling, especially if you're about to indulge in New Year's libations. Our family usually served ttok kuk with mandu, the chewy, soft ttok lying under the tasty dumplings.

You could add vegetables like bok choy, watercress, won bok, mustard greens or spinach to this dish. Or you could make ttok kuk with Oxtail Soup (page 26).

½ pound beef, round or sirloin
3 tablespoons Basic Korean Sauce (page 66)
2 teaspoons oil
6 pieces hind ttok
8 cups beef or chicken broth
4 green onions, chopped
Egg garnish (page 106; use 2 eggs)
2 sheets seaweed, crumpled
Sil kochu for garnish

Slice the beef into ¼-inch pieces then cut into fine strips. Place in a bowl and add the Basic Korean Sauce. Marinate for 30 minutes.

In a small skillet, heat the oil over medium high heat. Add the beef and cook until well done. Transfer to a bowl and set aside.

Slice the hind ttok into ⅜-inch thick pieces on the diagonal.

*continued on the next page*

Bring water to a boil in a medium saucepan.

Bring the broth to a boil in another saucepan; taste broth and adjust seasoning if needed. Reduce the heat, cover and keep hot.

When you are ready to serve, drop the sliced hind ttok into the boiling water. Cook for 2 to 3 minutes or until ttok is soft. Remove from the water with a slotted spoon and divide among 4 serving bowls. Sprinkle green onions and egg over the top. Add the hot broth. Top with beef and seaweed. Garnish with sil kochu. Serve at once.

# Yak Pap
# Steamed Sweet Rice

*Serves 8*

Yak pap, *also known as yak sik, is sticky, sweet, glutinous rice steamed with chestnuts, red dates, pine nuts and honey to make a confection that is quite addictive. It is often referred to as medicinal rice because of all the good things in the mixture.*

*The origin of this dish is linked to a legend about a crow that delivered a message to King Sochi, the twenty-first king of the Silla Dynasty. The King read the message then shot an arrow that killed his Queen and a monk who were embracing in a harp case. By doing so, the King escaped death that was being planned for him. Crow Thanksgiving Day was declared on the 15th day of the first moon; January 15 is celebrated with yak pap in honor of the crow.*

*Chestnuts, in season during the winter months, are prominent in this dish and are ideal when fresh, raw and peeled. The next best chestnuts are peeled frozen ones found in Korean supermarkets. Dried chestnuts will do, but require a long soaking (5 to 6 hours) before they can be mixed in. You could also use canned chestnuts, draining the syrup that comes with it.*

*My mother always made yak pap for the New Year celebration and I've continued the tradition!*

*continued on page 20*

**1 pound sweet or glutinous (mochi) rice, about 2⅓ cups**
**⅔ cup dried red dates**
**½ cup quartered peeled chestnuts, see note on page 18**
**3 tablespoons pine nuts**
**3 tablespoons soy sauce**
**¾ cup brown sugar**
**¼ cup honey**
**1 tablespoon sesame oil**

Soak the glutinous rice in water for several hours or overnight. Soak the red dates for 2 hours.

Drain the water and place the rice in a cheese-cloth-lined steamer. Steam over simmering water for 30 minutes.

Remove the pits from the red dates and if the dates are large, cut them into halves or quarters. Place dates, chestnuts and pine nuts in a large bowl.

Add the remaining ingredients to the bowl and mix together. When the rice is cooked, add it to the bowl and mix well. Return the mixture to the cheesecloth lined steamer and steam for about 3 hours, adding water to the steamer bottom as needed. Stir the mixture every 30 minutes. The rice will darken and become sticker with more time—both desirable qualities for yak pap. The chestnuts should be soft and sweet.

Serve warm or at room temperature. Yak pap may be refrigerated and reheated in a microwave; it can also be frozen and reheated.

# Silu Ttok
# Layered Rice Cake

*Makes about 100 pieces*

**A**gnes Rho Chun is a family friend, a second-generation Korean who is well known within the Korean community as an excellent Korean cook and teacher. She has experimented with many dishes over the years, reconstructing dishes that her mother made and modernizing the techniques. The following is a recipe she has perfected—a layered rice cake treat that few people make at home anymore. It was demonstrated in 1978 at a Hawaiian Electric Company community event celebrating the 75th anniversary of the immigration of Koreans to Hawai'i.

5 (10-ounce) packages rice flour
2 (10-ounce) packages sweet rice flour (mochiko)
2 teaspoons salt
4 cups boiling water
2½ cups sugar
2 pounds black eyed peas

In a large bowl, combine rice flour, mochiko and salt. Add boiling water all at once and mix with pastry blender. Add sugar and toss lightly. Cover and let stand for 1 hour.

In a large saucepan, cover peas with water so level of water is at least 2 inches above peas. Cover and bring to a full rolling boil; lower heat and simmer for about 25 minutes or until peas are soft but not mushy. Drain. Then let peas dry in a saucepan over very low heat, about 5 to 10 minutes, tossing frequently, until peas are dry and loose.

Mash peas. Consistency of the mashed peas should be loose; not mushy or sticky. If mushy or sticky, place in a large pan and dry out in the oven at 175 to 200°F Toss with spoon after 5 minutes or so and keep repeating until dry and loose.

Line a 13-inch round steaming pan with cheesecloth; place a layer of peas on cloth, then a layer of flour mixture. Repeat with 2 more layers of each, top with a layer of peas. Steam for 35 to 45 minutes. Allow cake to cool completely before removing from pan.

# Ttok Pokkum
# Rice Cake Stir-Fry
*Serves 4*

Ttok is Korean rice cake, like Japanese mochi, made of glutinous rice that is steamed then pounded into a smooth, chewy cake. Hind ttok is ttok that is shaped into a cylindrical log, about an inch in diameter and about 8 inches long. It is usually sliced on the diagonal and served in soup or stir fried with vegetables. A skinnier version is used to make ttok boki, a street food snack of rice cakes in a red spicy sauce.

I keep sliced hind ttok in my freezer and use it like pasta for a one-bowl meal. It takes just a few minutes in boiling water for the ttok to transform itself from frozen discs to soft, chewy rice cakes. Stir fry meat, mushrooms, greens and other vegetables, add the ttok and a few tablespoons of Basic Korean Sauce and you have a meal in a bowl. No rice cooker needed.

My aunt, Salome Han, often mentioned a ttok dish her mother made with meat, red dates, mushrooms and pine nuts. My aunt never made the dish but I've concocted one that has gotten good reviews from those who have eaten it. Add watercress or bok choy for a great meal in a bowl.

8 to 10 dried shiitake mushrooms, or fresh
½ cup dried red dates
½ pound beef, round or sirloin
6 tablespoons Basic Korean Sauce (page 66)
4 pieces hind ttok
4 green onions
1 tablespoon oil
3 tablespoons pine nuts

Soak the shiitake mushrooms in water until soft. Remove stems and cut the caps into thin strips. Set aside.

Soak the red dates for a couple of hours. When they are soft, cut them lengthwise and remove the pit. Slice each half into thin strips and set aside.

*continued on the next page*

Slice the beef into ¼-inch slices then cut into thin strips. Place in a bowl and add 2 tablespoons of the Basic Korean Sauce; marinate for 30 minutes.

Cut the hind ttok into diagonal slices, ⅜-inch thick; you should have about 2 cups. Cut the green onions into 1-inch pieces.

Bring a pot of water to a boil. Add the ttok slices and cook for 2 to 3 minutes, until soft. Drain and set aside.

Heat a large skillet or wok over high heat. Add a tablespoon of oil. Add the beef and stir-fry for 1 minute. Add the mushrooms, dates and ttok and stir-fry for 2 minutes. Add the remaining 4 tablespoons Basic Korean Sauce and continue to stir-fry for another 2 minutes; add a tablespoon or two of water if the mixture is too dry. Add the pine nuts and green onions, toss together and cook for 1 minute. Transfer to a serving dish and serve.

# Kuk & Tchigae
# Soups & Stews

Soup is vital to a Korean meal, although there is a fine line between a soup and stew. In Korean cooking both rely on a soupy base, and both probably evolved as a way of using up scraps. Stew probably has more ingredients but it is not necessarily thick, like Western stews. In Korean recipe books, few soups and stews are identical in their use of ingredients and seasonings.

I've learned that cooks in the Seoul area and the north generally use beef as the basis of their soups. In Pusan, the south, where seafood is abundant, fresh or dried fish, shrimp, clams, mussels and oysters add flavor.

Korean soups are generally water-based rather than stock-based. The ingredients and seasonings—usually a small amount of meat, garlic, vegetables and soy sauce—give flavor to the broth. Korean cooks use a special soup soy sauce—kuk kan jang—to add a little more depth of flavor.

I prefer a stock—beef, chicken, pork, seafood or vegetable—in my soups to add a more satisfying dimension of flavor. I like to make my own, boiling bones or vegetables for hours to release their essence. Canned stocks or broths, bouillon cubes and other stock bases also can be used. Whether you use water or stock, Korean soups are full of flavor.

# Kkori Komtang
## Oxtail Soup
### Serves 4

There was a time when oxtail was a throw-away, inexpensive cut of beef used only in ethnic dishes. To-day oxtail, like short ribs, has become a desirable cut among contemporary chefs who like to take lesser, non-prime cuts to show off their cooking talents. Like short ribs, oxtail has become a more expensive item with limited supply, but desirable for its flavor.

In Hawai'i, oxtails have always been prepared as Chinese-style soup with peanuts and stews flavored with star anise or black beans. After hours of cooking in water or braising in a well-seasoned broth, oxtail meat becomes very tender while still retaining good flavor. Koreans like to make soup with oxtails, very simply simmered for a long time to extract the rich, beefy flavor.

Oxtail soup should be prepared a day ahead of serving so you can refrigerate it overnight and remove the fat that will congeal. Most recipes will tell you to just put the oxtail pieces in a pot, add water and boil. But I find that browning the oxtail first then adding water will produce a deep brown broth with much more flavor.

You can serve this hearty soup with whole oxtails in the bowl or remove all the meat from the bones and serve the shredded pieces in the broth. I prefer to do it this way with rice, kimchi and other pickled vegetables alongside. Sometimes I'll serve the soup with pieces of hind ttok and added vegetables like bok choy or spinach for a meal in a bowl.

*Kuk & Tchigae*

1 tablespoon oil
4 to 5 pounds oxtails
12 cups water
5 cloves garlic, unpeeled
Salt or soy sauce, to taste
8 green onions, cut into 1-inch pieces

Place a wide, deep saucepan or a stockpot over medium high heat. Add the oil and when the oil is hot, add the oxtail pieces in one layer. Brown the oxtail pieces on all sides, taking your time to allow them to brown well, about 4 to 5 minutes per side. Do not let the oil or oxtail pieces burn; lower the heat if this starts to happen. When the pieces are browned, transfer them to a plate and continue to brown all the pieces.

When all the pieces are browned, pour off the oil in the pot. Add the water and return the oxtail pieces to the pot. Bring the water to a boil and skim any particles that rise to the top. Continue to skim as you reduce the heat to a simmer. Add the garlic cloves. Simmer for 4 to 5 hours, uncovered, or until oxtail meat is fork tender. Remove the pot from the heat and allow to cool.

Transfer the oxtails to a plate and cool. Reserve the larger pieces of oxtail for serving and strip the meat off the smaller pieces. Or strip the meat off all the oxtails for serving. Cover the meat and the oxtails and refrigerate.

Pour the broth through a fine strainer into another pot or a large bowl. Cool, cover and refrigerate overnight.

The next day, spoon off the fat that has congealed at the top of the broth and discard.

Heat the broth with oxtail pieces and meat. Season with salt or soy sauce to taste and bring to a boil. Add green onions. Ladle broth and oxtail into a serving bowl.

# Yukkaejang
## Spicy Beef Soup
*Serves 4*

When I was in the city of Daegu, I had a rich, flavorful soup for breakfast that was comforting and nourishing, a great way to start the day (though it would be just as good for lunch or dinner). This soup relies on a well-rendered beef stock, made from oxtails or bones with some meat thrown in. Then it needs a lot of leeks or green onions for more flavor. This recipe is based on what I remember and I believe resembles a soup called *Yukkaejang.*

- **8 ounces white radish (daikon)**
- **3 leeks or 10 green onions**
- **6 cups beef stock (page 158)**
- **2 cups cooked beef, shredded**
- **½ onion, sliced**
- **1 tablespoon minced garlic**
- **3 tablespoons soy sauce**
- **2 tablespoons kochu karu (chili pepper powder)**
- **2 teaspoons sesame oil**

Peel the radish and cut into bite-sized pieces; you should have about 2 cups. Clean the leeks, splitting them in half lengthwise and rinsing them well. Cut the halves again lengthwise, then cut into 1½-inch pieces crosswise. If using green onions, clean and cut into 1½-inch pieces.

Heat the stock in a large saucepan. Add the beef, radish, leeks, onion and garlic and bring to a boil. Reduce the heat and simmer for 20 minutes. Add the soy sauce, kochu karu and sesame oil and simmer for another 10 minutes. Taste and adjust seasoning, adding salt if needed. Ladle into bowls and serve with rice.

# Minari Kuk
# Watercress Soup

*Serves 6*

**W**hat we call watercress or minari in Hawai'i is not what minari is in Korea. No doubt our watercress was what was available to Korean cooks in the first half of the 20th century and they made soup with it that was flavorful and reminiscent of the soup in Korea.

Eldean Scott remembers how her mother, Hazel Pahk Chung, was meticulous about preparing the watercress for this soup: "Starting at the leafy end of the stem, we needed to pinch apart the stem between the leaf sheaf, about 2 inches long. We needed to be careful not to bruise or break the leaves. This was tedious work for a child and clearly taught patience. This is one of my favorite soups." Hazel Pahk Chung demonstrated this soup at a Hawaiian Electric Company class in 1987.

> 2 bunches watercress
> 1 tablespoon sesame oil
> 8 cups water
> 1½ pounds lean pork, thinly sliced
> 1 tablespoon salt
> 3 eggs, slightly beaten

Wash watercress and break into 2-inch pieces. Heat oil in a large saucepan. Add water and bring to a full rolling boil. Add the pork and simmer for 10 minutes. Stir in salt. Add watercress and bring to a boil again. Turn off heat and stir in eggs. Let stand for 1 minute before serving.

*Kuk & Tchigae*

# Kimchi Tchigae
# Kimchi Stew

*Serves 6*

This is a dish my mother often prepared, a comforting bowl of flavor and spice. Sour kimchi makes this soup especially flavorful. Use pork shoulder or pork belly; tofu is optional but makes this a heartier soup.

**4 ounces pork, cut into thin strips**
**1 teaspoon oil**
**2 cups pork stock or water**
**4 tablespoons toen jang (miso)**
**1 tablespoon kochu jang (chili pepper paste)**
**1 cup sour kimchi**
**12 ounces tubu (tofu), cut into 1 inch cubes**
**4 green onions, chopped**

In a medium saucepan over high heat, heat the oil. Add the pork and stir fry until browned. Add the pork broth. Mix in the toen jang and ko-chu jang and blend well. Add the kimchi and tofu and bring to a boil. Lower the heat and simmer for 20 minutes. Add the green on-ions and simmer for 2 minutes. Serve with rice.

# Miyok Kuk
# Seaweed Soup
## Serves 4

**M**iyok kuk is a classic Korean soup, tasty, soothing and full of good-for-you-seaweed. It is the traditional food served to mothers who have given birth, believed to restore their health. It is a soup that was a meal when I was growing up and one that I have happily rediscovered in doing this book.

Traditionally, this soup is made with water, producing a light soup. I like to use a hearty beef stock, adding depth of flavor. Joyce Lee, who came to Hawai'i in 1959 from the Pusan area of Korea, prepares miyok kuk with a dried shrimp-based stock. "Beef broth is used in Seoul, fish or seafood bases in Pusan," said Lee. Experimenting will no doubt bring delicious results.

Look for dried seaweed at Korean supermarkets, also known as wakame. Soak the seaweed in water for at least 30 minutes; seaweed will expand a lot when reconstituted—one ounce becomes 3 cups after soaking.

Diced tofu is sometimes added to this soup for more nourishment. For vegetarians, you can omit the beef.

1 ounce dried seaweed
1 tablespoon sesame oil
1 tablespoon minced garlic
4 ounces beef, cut into matchstick pieces
3 tablespoons soy sauce
6 cups beef stock (page 158) or water
2 green onions, chopped, for garnish

Soak seaweed in water for 30 minutes. Drain; cut seaweed into pieces that will fit a soup spoon.

In a large saucepan over medium heat, add the sesame oil, garlic and beef. Saute for a few minutes, until meat is cooked through. Add the seaweed, soy sauce and stock and bring to a boil. Reduce the heat to low, cover and simmer for 20 minutes. Ladle into soup bowls and garnish with green onions. Serve at once.

# Piji
# Soybean Dreg Stew

*Serves 2*

When you make soybean curd, the leftover solids that are separated from the liquid that gets molded into tofu is the whey, tofu lees or soybean dregs. It's a crumbly, grainy, bland product that is quite nutritious. The Japanese call it okara and usually add seasonings, carrot and gobo (burdock root) and eat it cold. The Koreans call it piji and it makes for a great stew-like dish.

I remember my dad bringing paper bags full of piji home like a prize find from the tofu factory where it was to be discarded or given to pig farmers. My mother would cook it with pork and sour kimchi; eaten over rice it is a hearty and delicious dish that is often overlooked today.

You can find piji at supermarkets but be sure to buy unseasoned versions. This is an excellent dish to use sour kimchi.

**3 ounces ground pork**
**8 ounces tofu lees**
**1 cup sour kimchi**
**2 cups pork stock or water**
**2 tablespoons (or more) kochu jang (chili pepper paste)**
**1 tablespoon soy sauce**
**2 green onions, coarsely chopped**

In a medium saucepan, brown the ground pork over medium high heat. Add the tofu lees, kimchi and water and mix together. Add the kochu jang and soy sauce and blend well. Bring to a boil; lower heat and simmer for 10 minutes. Add the green onions and cook an additional 2 minutes. Serve with hot rice.

# Kong Namul Kuk
# Soybean Sprout Soup

*This soup is often served alongside Pibimpap, the mixed rice bowl (page 12). It is a comforting soup; you could add slivers of beef or tofu to this soup.*

**8 ounces soybean sprouts**
**1 tablespoon sesame oil**
**1 tablespoon soy sauce**
**4 cups beef stock (page 158)**
**3 green onions, coarsely chopped**
**Salt to taste**

Clean the soybean sprout heads and trim the tails of each sprout. Rinse and drain.

In a saucepan, heat the sesame oil over medium heat. Add the soybean sprouts and cook for 2 minutes. Add the soy sauce and stock, bring to a boil. Reduce the heat and simmer for 5 to 8 minutes, until sprouts are tender. Add green onions; taste and adjust seasoning. Serve at once.

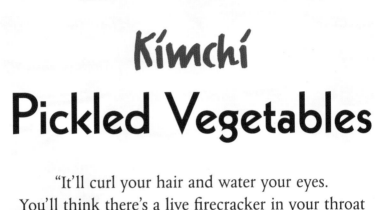

# Kimchi
# Pickled Vegetables

"It'll curl your hair and water your eyes.
You'll think there's a live firecracker in your throat
when it gets there, and your stomach will run around
the inside of you trying to get away from it.
But oh, how you love it."

—*Genie Pitchford,* Honolulu Advertiser, *October 3, 1953*

Kimchi, pickled vegetables, is the most relished and well-known dish of the Korean table, the national dish, the dish that must be served at every meal, and the dish, served with rice and soup, that constitutes a basic Korean meal.

The Korean diet is rich in vegetables, but the absence of fresh vegetables in winter led to the practice of preservation by drying or salting. The first records of kimchi made by salting appear around the seventh century. In the 1600s, paechu (won bok, Chinese or napa cabbage) and chili peppers were found in Korea, but it wasn't until the 1800s that kimchi as

we know it today, made from paechu and spiced with chili peppers, was widely made.

Kimchi—originally called chimchae, or soaked vegetables—is like tsukemono in Japanese cuisine or sauerkraut in German, both salt-preserved vegetables, except kimchi has more flavor and spice. In Korea, juicy, milder, more delicately seasoned kimchi is characteristic of the north, where cooler climates helped preserve the vegetables. In the warmer south, kimchi is more pungent; salt and fermented seafood products are employed to preserve as well as flavor the vegetables. Kim jang, the seasonal preparation of kimchi for the winter, continues today, even though refrigeration and the availability of fresh vegetables makes kimchi available all year.

Kimchi is considered a very healthy food, low in calories, a good source of dietary fiber and vitamins A, B-complex and C; and of calcium, iron and phosphorus. If salted seafood such as shrimp, oysters or fish are part of the kimchi mix, protein is supplied as well, thus it can be a meal in itself. The living microbes—probiotics—produced during the fermentation and maturation process are helpful in maintaining a healthy digestive track. Kimchi also is said to help strengthen bones and prevent cancer.

Good kimchi is a dish of balance: enough salt to prevent the loss of crispness and spoilage, tastiness provided by garlic, green onions, salted seafood and overall spiciness. Kimchi should not be too salty, too fishy or to spicy; it should be crisp and crunchy and provide a mouthful of savoriness that is delicious.

# Kimchi in Hawai'i

When Koreans came to Hawai'i in the early 1900s, they brought kimchi with them. It has become a very popular dish in the islands, appearing on any buffet table at any gathering, no matter the ethnic background of the family. No doubt the saltiness, pungency and spiciness that define kimchi are appealing in a place where bold flavors are preferred. And in Hawai'i, kimchi is its own unique dish, different from its homeland counterpart.

The first company to make and sell kimchi in Hawai'i was Joe Kim's. Joe was the oldest son of Chin Wha and Theresa So Chun Kim, he an immigrant sugar plantation worker, she his picture bride. The family grew won bok in Kalihi Valley in the 1930s. One day, a freak hailstorm damaged the crop and Joe suggested that his mother make kimchi with the cabbage that could be salvaged. Theresa Kim did just that and began peddling her kimchi to vegetable stands. Eventually they bottled the kimchi under the name Diamond Kimchi, later renamed Joe Kim's.

In 1949, Hannah Liu founded Kohala Kimchi in Kapa'au on the island of Hawai'i. Kea'au Kimchi, started by Ya Mul Kim, began at about the same time on the opposite side of the island. In 1955 Helen Halm started Halm's Kimchi and expanded her market to the U.S. mainland.

These four brands dominated the Hawai'i market for years, each with a distinct flavor profile and loyal following. Island-style kimchi is generally more watery and salty, but not as spicy and without some of the seafood flavors that make up authentic Korean kimchi.

Perhaps it's the influence of Japanese tsukemono (salted vegetables) on local palates that has shaped island kimchi. That's the theory of Mike Irish, known as Hawai'i's "kimchi king" because he owns seven kimchi brands under the Halm's Enterprises umbrella. "Kimchi that is sweeter has a shorter shelf life and turns sour faster," says Irish. "Kimchi and tsukemono were close and it became a blended product."

Irish began his foray into the Korean food business in 1984 when he bought Park's brand Korean sauces. Park's kimchi sauce was favored by many cooks at the growing number of hostess bars in Honolulu. One bar owner/cook was Alice Yang, better known as Chicken Alice for the spicy, crispy chicken wings she made popular in the 1980s and 1990s. She used the Park's sauce, ordered by the gallons, and encouraged Irish to buy the company.

A year later Irish bought Halm's Kimchi and subsequently acquired six other kimchi brands from the families that had started them: Kohala, Kewalo, Sweet Charley, Man Nani, A-1 and High Max.

From a central Kalihi manufacturing facility, Irish processes more than three tons of island-grown won bok, cucumber, daikon and head cabbage into kimchi every day. "I want to preserve the flavors of the original companies," says Irish, who maintains the cut size of the vegetables, salting processes and seasonings for each brand. "Fresh-to-market is the philosophy; I want to provide a crispy, fresh product to the consumer."

Irish is a third-generation Korean-American whose grandmother was a picture bride. "There was always a gallon of kimchi in the refrigerator and my after-school snack was a kimchi sandwich."

Ah, yes, kimchi on white bread with a little mayonnaise was a childhood favorite. Perhaps this was the first Korean fusion dish! Today, of course, kimchi tops hot dogs, is mixed into hamburgers, replaces sauerkraut in Reuben-style sandwiches, is included in fried rice, mixed with cream cheese for a dip … there's even a kimchi Portuguese sausage.

Certainly Edwin Noh played a role in the popularization of kimchi. In 1961 Noh and his wife Miriam opened Arirang Korean restaurant where, as in any Korean restaurant, kimchi

DeSoto Brown Collection

was a staple. Workers made 60 pounds every day, spending hours soaking cabbage and peeling and chopping garlic and ginger. Noh decided there had to be a better and faster way.

He began experimenting with dehydrated ingredients and in 1965 offered for sale a packaged dehydrated kimchi sauce mix, the first of many mixes and sauces that he would develop for popular ethnic dishes. With Noh's kimchi mix, you chop the cabbage, soak it in salt water, drain it and add the mix. Instant kimchi!

Hundreds of varieties of kimchi are made in Korea with almost any vegetable. The most popular type worldwide is made with pae-chu or won bok. In Hawai'i, cucumber, white radish and head cabbage kimchi are popular, too.

# Kimchi Party Dip

*Makes about 1 quart*

A cookbook about Korean food in Hawai'i would not be complete without this recipe. It's one of those "only in Hawai'i" things, concocted by someone who liked kimchi and cream cheese, the latter being the perfect foil for anything spicy. What could be simpler and tastier with chips? Here's a recipe from The Honolulu Advertiser, 1976.

**½ cup chopped kimchi**
**1 tablespoon kimchi juice**
**1 (8-ounce) package cream cheese, quartered**

Put all ingredients into blender; cover and blend 1 minute. Chill; serve with chips or fresh vegetables.

# Paechu Kimchi
# Won Bok Kimchi

*Makes about 1 quart*

This is the classic kimchi, made with won bok or Napa cabbage, made for centuries and embraced the world over. It is delicious fresh, soured over a few days and even well fermented. There are many ways to enjoy this treasured Korean dish.

1 head won bok, about 2 pounds
2 tablespoons salt
2 cloves garlic, finely minced
1 teaspoon finely minced ginger
¼ cup green onion, about 2 stalks
2 tablespoons kochu karu (chili pepper powder)
1 tablespoon fish sauce

Remove outer leaves of won bok and rinse. Cut won bok crosswise in 2-inch pieces. Place won bok in a large bowl, sprinkle with salt and toss together. Let stand for 3 to 4 hours or until won bok is wilted and has lost some of its crunchiness.

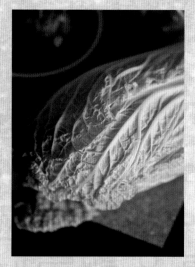

Drain the won bok in a colander and rinse, tossing well under the water to remove the salt. Drain and return won bok to large bowl.

Add the remaining ingredients to the won bok and mix well. Pack kimchi into a jar and cover. Let stand on kitchen countertop for a day before refrigerating. If you want your kimchi to sour quickly, do not refrigerate but leave on the counter. Within a couple of days the kimchi will turn sour.

# Oi Kimchi
# Stuffed Cucumber Kimchi
*Makes about 1 quart*

A classic kimchi, popular for its crunchiness, especially when made with Japanese variety cucumbers. This recipe is from a 1978 Hawaiian Electric cooking demonstration.

3 long slender cucumbers
1 tablespoon plus 2 teaspoons salt
1 cup minced chives
1 tablespoon grated carrot
1 to 1½ tablespoon kochu karu (chili pepper powder)
1 tablespoon water
1 teaspoon minced garlic
½ teaspoon minced ginger
1 tablespoon minced pine nuts
2 teaspoons sugar

Cut cucumbers into uniform 1-inch pieces. Make 2 slashes, like a cross, about ½-inch down in each piece. Sprinkle with 1 tablespoon salt and let stand for 30 minutes. Drain well.

Combine remaining ingredients and stuff each cucumber piece with mixture. Place in jar, cover, and let stand at room temperature for 4 to 5 hours to ripen. Store in refrigerator.

*Kimchi*

# Tongchimi
# White Radish Kimchi

*Makes about 1 quart*

*Crisp white radish kimchi is so refreshing, often served at the beginning of a meal to whet your appetite. The juice from this kimchi is perfect for making the dish of cold noodles called naengmyun (page 111).*

**1 large white radish, about 2 pounds**
**5 teaspoons salt**
**1 clove garlic, peeled and sliced thin**
**2⅛-inch thick, quarter-size slices ginger, peeled**
**1 teaspoon sugar**
**1 small red chili pepper, thinly sliced into rounds**
**5 cups water**

Peel radish and slice into ¼-inch thick pieces. Place in a bowl and sprinkle with 3 teaspoons of the salt; mix well. Let stand for 20 minutes. Rinse well and place in a covered container. Add the remaining 2 teaspoons of salt, garlic, ginger, sugar and chili pepper. Pour the 5 cups of water over, stir a little to mix. Cover and refrigerate for 2 days.

# Kkaktugi
# White Radish Kimchi

*Makes 2 quarts*

Kkaktugi is kimchi made with white radish, often called turnip, cut into bite-sized cubes and seasoned. It always looks spicier than it really is; crunch is what this kimchi is all about. This recipe is from the Hawaiian Electric Company's collection of Korean recipes, circa 1976.

   5 pounds white radish
   4 quarts water
   1 cup rock salt
   ¼ cup sugar
   2 tablespoons minced garlic
   1½ teaspoons paprika
   1½ tablespoons minced ginger
   1½ teaspoons kochu karu (chili pepper powder)
   ½ teaspoon MSG (optional)
   1 tablespoon sugar

Pare and cut turnips crosswise into thirds, then lengthwise into quarters. Combine water, salt and sugar in a large bowl. Put turnips into water mixture and place a weighted plate on top to keep them submerged. Soak for 6 hours. Rinse turnips 5 times in cold water. Drain and put into jars. Combine remaining ingredients and pour over turnips. Let stand at room temperature for 2 days, then refrigerate.

# Chon
# Pan-Fried Foods

**M**eats, fish and vegetables, sliced and seasoned, dipped in flour and egg, then pan-fried—this is chon. It's a simple preparation and one that shouldn't be limited to a Korean meal.

Everything is a candidate for this cooking technique. Zucchini, eggplant, green pepper, meat and fish are traditional. But consider fresh mushrooms, slices of broccoli and cauliflower, cooked sweet potato, carrots, leeks, asparagus and green beans. Serve chon with table sauces.

For a meal, I like to prepare chon well before guests arrive; serving it at room temperature is fine. You can keep chon warm in a 200°F oven or a warming drawer if you like.

The recipes here are for a small quantity of each item; if you're cooking for a crowd you'll want to increase the quantities. In a Korean meal, chon is but one of many side dishes and the more the merrier.

# Kaji
# Eggplant

*Serves 4 as a side dish*

Like zucchini, eggplant chon is simple to prepare and delicious. Use the long Japanese eggplant, cut into round or diagonal slices. These eggplant tend to be less bitter than the large globe eggplants. You can use the globe eggplant but sprinkle with salt and let stand for 15 minutes, rinse and pat dry before cooking. A large long eggplant will yield about 15 slices, enough to serve 4 as a side dish.

**1 large eggplant, Japanese variety preferred**
**2 tablespoons flour**
**1 egg**
**Oil for frying**
**Salt**

Wash eggplant and remove the ends. Cut eggplant into ⅜-inch slices.

Place the flour in a shallow bowl. Break egg into another bowl and beat.

Heat a skillet over medium high heat. Coat the eggplant slices in the flour. Dip eggplant in egg. Add oil to coat the skillet and when it is hot, place the eggplant slices in the pan. Sprinkle with salt. Fry the eggplant until golden brown then turn each piece and brown the other side. With a fork, test for doneness; the eggplant should be soft. Transfer to a paper towel-lined plate. Continue to fry until all the pieces are cooked, adding more oil if needed. Serve at room temperature.

# Hobak
# Zucchini
*Serves 4 as a side dish*

*Z*ucchini chon is simply terrific even if you're not serving Korean food. I like to keep the pieces on the thick side and I like to cook them quickly so that the texture is a little "crunchy" rather than well done and soft. One medium zucchini will yield about 15 pieces, enough to serve 4 people as a side dish. This is, of course an approximation, and leftover zucchini chon is always delicious straight from the refrigerator!

A tip: When making a variety or quantity of chon, especially vegetables, place flour in a gallon-size plastic bag. Add the vegetables and shake to coat with flour.

**1 medium zucchini**
**2 tablespoons flour**
**1 egg**
**Salt**
**Oil for frying**

Wash zucchini and remove the ends. Cut zucchini into 3/8-inch slices. Place flour in a shallow bowl. Break egg in another bowl and beat.

Heat a skillet over medium high heat. Coat zucchini slices in flour. Dip zucchini in egg to coat. Add oil to coat the skillet and when it is hot, place the zucchini slices in the pan. Sprinkle with salt. Fry the zucchini until golden brown then turn each piece and brown the other side. With a fork, test for doneness; the zucchini should be somewhat firm but tender. Transfer to a paper towel-lined plate. Continue to fry until all pieces are cooked, adding more oil if needed. Serve at room temperature.

# Saengson Fish

*Serves 6 as a side dish*

Fresh caught island fish is ideal for making fish chon, a simple preparation for a side dish or pūpū. I like to use mahimahi, nairage and 'ahi tombo for fish chon. Cook this over high heat so the egg browns quickly and you don't overcook the fish.

1 pound fish
1 tablespoon sesame oil
1 teaspoon salt
3 tablespoons flour
2 eggs
Oil for frying

Cut the fish into ⅜-inch thick slices. Lay the slices on a plate. Brush each piece with sesame oil and sprinkle with salt. Sprinkle flour over the fish and coat each piece in flour.

In a bowl, beat the eggs. Dip the fish into the egg and coat well. Heat a skillet over high heat. Add a tablespoon of oil and when it is hot, add the fish pieces to the pan. Brown the fish pieces and turn to brown the other side. Brief cooking is all that is required. Transfer to a paper towel-lined plate. Continue to fry until all pieces are cooked, adding more oil if needed. Serve at room temperature.

# Kogi
# Beef

*Serves 4 as a side dish*

According to several people in the Korean food business and to people from Korea, meat chon as it is served in Hawai'i is unique to Hawai'i. I've always considered it a part of my Korean repertoire but it is not a preparation found in Korea nor in Los Angeles, where the largest Korean immigrant population resides.

In Korea, meat chon is made as individual, small pieces of meat, seasoned with salt and pepper, dipped in flour and egg and pan-fried. It is not marinated in soy sauce-garlic-sesame oil as it is in Hawai'i. Perusing several Korean cookbooks, you will not find a recipe for Hawai'i's meat chon.

People in Hawai'i love beef chon as a side dish, pūpū or even an entrée. There's good reason to like this dish: well-seasoned meat, coated in egg and quickly pan-fried is delicious!

Be sure to coat each piece of meat well with flour and egg to encase the marinade that will inevitably ooze out and make your frying pan sticky. Some Korean cooks do a double coat, dipping in flour and egg twice to encase the meat and seasonings.

**½ pound top round or sirloin**
**2 tablespoons Basic Korean Sauce (page 66)**
**2 tablespoons flour**
**2 eggs**
**Oil for frying**

Slice meat thin, about ¼-inch. Place in a bowl and add the sauce; marinate for about an hour.

Place flour in a shallow bowl. Beat eggs in a shallow bowl. Coat each slice of beef in flour, then dip in egg to coat well.

Heat a skillet over medium high heat. Add 2 tablespoons of oil to the skillet and when it is hot, add the meat to the pan. Brown the meat and turn to brown the other side. Transfer to a paper towel-lined plate. Continue to fry until all the pieces are cooked, adding more oil if needed. Serve hot or at room temperature.

# Zucchini and Ground Beef

*Serves 6 as a side dish*

'm not sure if this is traditional but it does taste good: a combination of zucchini and ground beef in a pan-fried "sandwich." It does require some work but it's a terrific side dish or *pūpū*.

**½ pound ground beef**
**1½ tablespoons Basic Korean Sauce (page 66)**
**2 medium zucchini**
**3 tablespoons flour**
**2 eggs**
**Oil for frying**

In a bowl, mix ground beef and sauce, combining well.

Cut zucchini into ¼-inch slices. Place about 2 teaspoons of ground beef on a slice of zucchini; top with another zucchini slice and press together.

Place flour in a shallow bowl. Beat eggs in another bowl. Coat each "sandwich" in flour then dip in egg.

Heat a skillet over medium heat. Add oil to coat the skillet and when it is hot, add the "sandwiches" to the pan. Brown the "sandwiches" and turn to brown the other side. Transfer to a paper towel-lined plate. Continue to fry until all the "sandwiches" are cooked, adding more oil if needed. Serve hot or at room temperature.

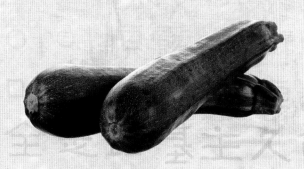

# Nrum Juk
## Skewered Meat and Vegetable

*Serves 8 to 10 as a side dish*

**M**y mother would always make nrum juk for the New Year celebration. It would require having kimchi made from won bok that was split in half lengthwise rather than cut into pieces. The kimchi had to be sour, of course. She would cut the kimchi into lengthwise strips, about ¾-inch wide.

Green onions, long strips of seasoned meat, celery and the kimchi would be threaded onto bamboo skewers (that was my job), alternating each ingredient. Each skewer, about 8 by 10 inches, would be coated well in flour then dipped in egg and pan-fried. After frying, the whole piece would be deftly cut into smaller pieces, about 3 inches square, and arranged on a serving platter. They were consumed with gusto.

If you can get the uncut won bok kimchi, prepare nrum juk as my mother did. With regular won bok kimchi, cut the ingredients to the same size and skewer the ingredients onto toothpicks. Either way, the combination of meat and vegetables is divine.

**1 pound beef, sirloin or top round, cut into ¾-inch strips**
**4 tablespoons Basic Korean Sauce (page 66)**
**½ whole won bok kimchi, cut into ¾-inch strips**
**6 to 8 pieces celery, cut into ¾-inch strips**
**24 green onions**
**Flour**
**12 eggs**
**Oil for frying**

Mix beef strips with sauce, using a tablespoon of sauce for every 4 ounces of beef. Marinate for a half hour.

Using bamboo skewers, thread the meat, kimchi, celery and green onion, alternating ingredients and placing each item very close together.

*continued on the next page*

Place flour in a wide shallow pan. Beat eggs in another wide pan. Coat each skewer in flour well. Dip in egg and coat well.

Heat a large skillet over medium high heat. Add oil to coat the skillet and when it is hot, add one of the skewers, laying it flat and arranging the ends so they are squared at the bottom. Fry until golden brown. Turn and cook the other side. Transfer to a paper towel-lined plate. Repeat frying, adding more oil as need.

Remove the skewer and place chon on a cutting board. Cut the chon into pieces, about 3-inches square. Arrange on a serving platter and serve at room temperature.

---

# Korean-Style Meatballs

*Serves 6 as a side dish*

Meatballs for pūpūs? Make them Korean style! It's hard to resist these tasty mouthfuls.

**1 pound ground beef**
**3 tablespoons Basic Korean Sauce (page 66)**
**3 tablespoons flour**
**2 eggs**
**Oil for frying**

In a bowl, mix ground beef and sauce, combining well. Shape the beef into 1-inch balls or small patties.

Place flour in a shallow bowl. Beat eggs in another bowl. Coat the meat balls well in flour then dip in egg to coat.

Heat a skillet over medium high heat. Add 2 tablespoons of oil to the skillet and when it is hot, add the meatballs to the pan. Brown the meatballs and turn to brown the other side. Transfer to a paper towel-lined plate. Continue to fry until all the meatballs are cooked, adding more oil if needed. Serve hot or at room temperature.

# Pindaettok
# Mung Bean Pancake
*Makes about 15 pieces; serves 4 as a side dish*

Pindaettok is a patty of pulverized mung beans with various vegetables and meats added, depending on the cook. It is often served up in stalls on the streets of Seoul, crisp and tasty.

In my family we like to make pindaettok with kimchi, pork and green onions. We like to soak and grind our beans in a blender or food processor and we add egg to our mixture. Most traditional recipes and today's cooks simply use mung bean powder, available in Korean supermarkets.

½ cup split mung beans
2 eggs
1 cup sour kimchi
4 ounces (about ½ cup) ground
  pork
3 green onions, chopped
½ teaspoon salt
Oil for frying

Soak mung beans in water for 3 to 4 hours; they will expand to about 1½ cups. Drain, then place mung beans in a blender or food processor with eggs and purée. Transfer to a bowl.

Chop the kimchi coarsely and squeeze out as much liquid as possible. Place in the bowl with the mung beans; add pork, green onions and salt and mix well.

Heat a skillet over medium heat. Add oil to coat the skillet and when it is hot, add the mung bean mixture by the spoonful, forming small patties, about 3 inches in diameter. Cook until golden brown, about 2 to 3 minutes. Flip to the other side and cook. Transfer to a paper towel-lined plate. Keep warm or serve at room temperature.

# Pa Chon I
# Green Onion Pancake I
*Serves 4 as a side dish*

**K**orean pancakes—chive, green onion, seafood—are a popular dish at many of today's Korean restaurants in Hawai'i. It is not a dish I grew up on except for kimchi pancakes which were made to use up sour kimchi.

The traditional Korean pancakes are made using a wheat flour mix available in Korean supermarkets; the mix is seasoned with salt, pepper, sugar and onion powder. Water is added to the mix, you mix in the vegetables or other ingredients and pan fry it into a large pancake. As the first side cooks, seafood bits are placed on the uncooked side; when the first side is nicely browned and cooked, you flip it over and cook the other side. The pancake is cut into wedges and served with a flavorful and spicy table sauce.

The texture of these pancakes is chewy and a lot of the flavor depends on the table sauce. I prefer to make my pancakes with flour and egg, seasoning the pancake with salt so that the pancake itself is flavorful on its own and a table sauce gives it an extra kick.

Here are two versions of chive or green onion pancakes, one using the mix, the other my version. You can make these pancakes with whatever you may have in your pantry: green beans, carrots, onions, broccoli, clams, oysters, shrimp, fish, meat, pork, chicken—two, three or four items will make for a tasty pancake.

**1 cup green onion or chives**
**½ cup Korean pancake mix**
**⅔ cup water**
**Seafood such as shrimp, clam, oysters (optional)**
**Oil for frying**

Cut the green onion or chives into 2-inch lengths. If you're using green onions, cut the white part lengthwise into strips.

In a bowl, whisk together the pancake mix and water until smooth. Add the chives or green onions and mix together.

Heat a 10-inch skillet over medium high heat. Add oil to coat the pan well. When the oil is hot, pour in the pancake mixture and flatten it into a round pancake, about 8 inches in diameter. If using, place seafood over the pancake. Reduce the heat to medium and cook until browned, about 3 to 4 minutes. Flip the pancake over and continue to cook for 3 to 4 minutes. Transfer to a plate. Cut into wedges and serve with a table sauce (pages 117-121).

---

# Pa Chon II
# Green Onion Pancake with Egg
*Serves 4 as a side dish*

**1 cup green onions or chives**
**2 tablespoons flour**
**2 eggs**
**½ teaspoon Kosher salt**
**Sil kochu (chili pepper thread, optional)**

Cut the green onion or chives into 2-inch lengths. If you're using green onions, cut the white part lengthwise into strips.

In a bowl, whisk the eggs until well beaten. Add the flour and blend together. Add the salt and the chives or green onions and mix together well.

Heat a 10-inch skillet over medium high heat. Add oil to coat the pan well. When the oil is hot, pour in the pancake mixture and flatten it into a round pancake, about 8 inches in diameter. If using, sprinkle sil kochu over the surface of the pancake. Reduce the heat to medium and cook until browned, about 3 to 4 minutes. Flip the pancake over and continue to cook for 3 to 4 minutes. Transfer to a plate. Cut into wedges and serve with a table sauce (page 117-121).

# Kimchi Chon
# Kimchi Pancake

*Serves 6 as a side dish*

Kimchi pancake is my favorite in the repertoire of chon that I make. I'm not sure that it is very traditional but it has been a part of my cooking for as long as I can remember. This is really about using sour kimchi, the kimchi that has been in the refrigerator for weeks, fully fermented and very sour to the taste. Pan-frying it this way is terrific.

**2 cups sour kimchi**
**4 green onions, cut into ½-inch pieces**
**2 tablespoons flour**
**2 eggs**
**Oil for frying**

Drain the kimchi, then coarsely chop. Squeeze the kimchi by the handful, pressing out as much liquid as possible. Place in a bowl. Add the green onions, flour and eggs and mix well.

Heat a skillet over medium high heat. Add oil to coat the skillet and when it is hot, drop spoonfuls of the kimchi mixture into the pan. Spread the mixture into a small pancake, about 3 inches in diameter. Fry until golden brown then turn and cook the other side. Transfer to a paper towel-lined plate. Serve hot or at room temperature.

# Kogi & Haemul
# Meats & Seafood

Beef, pork, chicken, fish and shellfish are all important within a Korean meal. Well seasoned proteins are barbecued, steamed, braised and sautéed, served in ample but not large quantities alongside rice, kimchi, soup and of course, panchan. A Korean meal offers variety in flavors and textures and a balance of protein, vegetables and starch.

# Beef Cuts in Korean Cooking

For one reason or another beef has become the significant protein in Korean cuisine (versus fish in Japan, pork in China). It's not that Korea had an abundance of beef throughout history or that pork, fish and seafood are not also prominent. But the renown of beef dishes like kalbi and pulkogi have certainly made Korean food famous.

Kalbi, grilled or braised, is made from short ribs, a cut from the chuck of the animal, a rib bone that has layers of fat and meat attached. This cut is not particularly tender and requires slow cooking to soften the muscle fibers. Or it needs to be cut in a way that makes it more tender.

In my family, short ribs, rectangles of about 2 by 3 inches, were marked with half-inch crosscuts, resulting in a checkerboard-like piece of meat still attached to the bone. This would allow the marinade to flavor the meat well; when it was grilled you would bite off a piece of the "checkerboard" that had browned well on all of its surfaces.

As Korean restaurants opened in Honolulu, kalbi was served in a different way. Short rib pieces were butterflied so the meat opened like a book, known as tong kalbi. Sometimes the kalbi was not marinated but just seasoned with salt and pepper.

Then came what's known as the LA cut or LA kalbi, born in Los Angeles, home of the largest population of Koreans outside Korea. The rib is sliced thin (no more than ¼-inch) across the bone; the 6-to 8-inch strip with three small bones on one side is the LA cut, the most popular short rib cut today. Not only is it served in restaurants, it is available in all supermarkets in Hawai'i. It's actually difficult to find the old-style, thick chuck short rib these days.

The LA cut offers a greater surface area for the marinade to bathe the meat. Its thinness means it will be more tender and will cook in a shorter time. The downside is that butchers lose on this cut as the ribs must be frozen, thawed and frozen again to make it possible to cut the thin strips.

Boneless short ribs have also come into vogue, just like boneless poultry, pork and fish. But save me the ones with the bones, please; gnawing on a piece of perfectly cooked kalbi is a pleasure, thank you!

When it comes to braised short ribs, kalbi tchim, the uncut, thick short rib is the one to use. Slow braising in a seasoned liquid makes it falling-off-the-bone tender.

Short ribs were not always popular in American cooking. But from the 1990s on, with chefs on a quest to utilize beef cuts other than steaks, short ribs became desirable. Chefs could show off their talents, slow-cooking short ribs to tender perfection, serving them in fine-dining venues for top prices. This has put a demand on short ribs (and other lesser beef cuts), making supplies and prices more dear.

Meats in the Korean repertoire are lean and tend to be the lesser, non-prime cuts that were inexpensive to a population that couldn't afford other parts of the animal. Also prominent cuts in Korean supermarkets:

* Sliced ribeye, a boneless, tender cut from the rib section, used in pulkogi, barbecued beef. The thin pieces are marinated and grilled.

* Beef brisket, cut from the breast section of the beef cow, used to make spicy beef soup (yukkaejang), braised in soy sauce for changjorim or thin-sliced for yakiniku, the Japanese term for grilling at the table.

* Shank, also used for changjorim.

* The flap cut, or skirt steak, grilled yakiniku-style or stewed.

* Oxtails, used to make a flavorful, rich soup with lots of green onions, are another cut that has suffered from popularity. This once-throwaway item now comes at a premium price, as chefs use it in various preparations.

Of course many more cuts are available in all our supermarkets and other cuts can be used in Korean dishes. Flank steak marinated in a Korean barbecue sauce, grilled and sliced thin, is a terrific pulkogi alternative as is sliced chuck steak. Prime steak cuts like sirloin, ribeye, Spencer and New York all benefit from a Basic Korean Sauce marinade. Stews flavored with Basic Korean Sauce also are delicious. It's all about the sauce!

# Basic Korean Sauce

*Makes 1 cup*

When it comes to basics in Korean cooking, this basic sauce does wonders. It's a marinade for kalbi, pulkogi, chicken, and sliced beef for chon; a seasoning for chap chae and other vegetable dishes; and a base for a table sauce. Of course, everyone has their own version and proportion of ingredients. This is my version, on the savory side with a sweet balance. If you like your Korean food sweeter, add more honey or sugar.

This recipe is based on using Kikkoman soy sauce. Soy sauces differ in flavor, density and saltiness so the cook should adjust accordingly.

- ⅔ **cup soy sauce**
- ⅓ **cup water**
- 1 **tablespoon minced garlic**
- ⅓ **cup sugar**
- 2 **tablespoons sesame oil**
- 2 **tablespoons roasted sesame seeds**
- ¼ **cup finely chopped green onions**

Measure all ingredients in a bowl and whisk together. Taste and adjust seasoning, adding more honey or sugar if desired.

---

# Kalbi Tchim I
# Braised Short Ribs I

*Serves 4*

Braised short ribs are delicious, tender, falling off the bone, well-seasoned, and perfect with steaming hot rice. Until I took a Korean cooking class in Korea, I always prepared this dish "Western" style, browning the short rib pieces, then adding the liquid and seasonings for braising. Traditional Korean style is a little different. I think both versions are tasty; try this recipe and the one that follows.

*A tip: It's a good idea to braise the short ribs one day and serve it the next. Refrigerating the dish overnight will allow the fat to congeal and you can easily remove it. If you're serving it the day you are making it, skim some of the fat off the top before serving.*

**3 pounds thick cut short ribs**
**2 tablespoons oil**
**½ cup Basic Korean Sauce (page 66)**
**3 cups beef stock (page 158) or water**
**1 small white radish**
**1 carrot**
**Chopped green onions for garnish**

Use a saucepan that is deep and wide that will hold the short rib pieces in one layer. Heat over medium high setting; add the oil. When the oil is hot, add the short ribs and cook about 3 to 5 minutes. When they are nicely browned and crusty, turn them over and cook the other side. Transfer the short ribs to a plate and drain the oil from the pan.

Place the saucepan back on the burner and add the Basic Korean Sauce and the stock. Bring to a boil, scraping any bits from the bottom of the pan. Return the short ribs to the pan. Reduce the heat to low, cover the pan and simmer for 1½ hours.

Peel the radish and carrot and cut into bite-size chunks. Add to the short ribs and cook, uncovered. Continue to cook until the vegetables are soft and the meat is fork tender. Leaving the cover off will reduce the liquid and concentrate the flavor a little.

When the meat and vegetables are cooked, serve at once over hot rice, garnishing with green onions. If you want the sauce to be thicker, make a slurry of 2 tablespoons each cornstarch and water. Remove the short ribs and vegetables with a slotted spoon. Bring the liquid to a boil and add the cornstarch slurry; cook for 1 minute. Return the short ribs and vegetables to the pan and cook together for another minute. Serve at once.

# Kalbí Tchím II
# Braised Short Ribs II
*Serves 4*

This is a more traditional version of braised short ribs, a recipe that I learned when I took a class at Ongo Food in Seoul on Royal Court Cuisine. It is a more delicately flavored dish, subtler in its seasonings but every bit as delicious as the version I have made for years. This recipe also employs some techniques that are basic to Korean cooking but unfamiliar to Western cooks.

3 pounds beef short ribs, thick cut with bone
1 carrot
1 small white radish
1 onion
2 to 3 whole dried red chili peppers
6 whole chestnuts, peeled

_Sauce:_
½ cup soy sauce
2 tablespoons rice wine
2 tablespoons sugar
2 tablespoons honey
4 teaspoons minced garlic
2 tablespoons minced green onion
¼ cup grated Asian pear

Remove excess fat and gristle from the short ribs. Soak the short ribs in cold water for 1 hour; this removes the blood.

Cut carrot and radish into 1½-inch chunks. Using a paring knife, pare the cut corners of each piece so they are rounded; you should have rounded pieces of carrot and radish. Cut the onion into 8 pieces.

Drain the short ribs and place in a saucepan. Add water to cover and place over high heat and bring to a boil. Boil for 3 to 5 minutes, allowing scum to rise to the surface. Remove from heat, drain and

*continued on the next page*

rinse. Clean the pan and return short ribs to the pan. Cover with fresh water and place over high heat.

Mix all the sauce ingredients and add to the pan. Add the carrots, radish, onion, chili peppers and chestnuts. Bring to a boil, reduce the heat to medium and cook, covered, for about 2 hours or until the meat is fork tender. If there is a lot of liquid, remove the cover and bring to a boil to reduce and thicken the sauce.

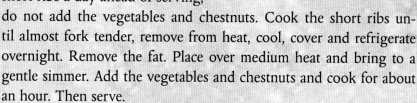

**Note:** If you are braising the short ribs a day ahead of serving, do not add the vegetables and chestnuts. Cook the short ribs until almost fork tender, remove from heat, cool, cover and refrigerate overnight. Remove the fat. Place over medium heat and bring to a gentle simmer. Add the vegetables and chestnuts and cook for about an hour. Then serve.

---

### Kalbi
# Barbecued Beef Short Ribs

*U se the LA cut of short ribs or the square, thick cut chuck short rib, cutting the meat to the bone in a checkerboard fashion. Marinate the about 4 pounds of short ribs in one recipe of Basic Korean Sauce (page 66) for 3 to 4 hours.*

*Heat a charcoal or gas grill. For the thinner LA cut short ribs, grill over medium high until nicely browned. For thicker short ribs, grill over medium heat to desired doneness, usually medium rare and nicely browned.*

# Changjorim
# Soy Braised Beef Cubes

*Serves 6 as a side dish*

changjorim is a dish of beef cubes stewed in soy sauce. It's tender, flavored with mild and hot green peppers, and salty. Just a little morsel of meat with rice was how we ate it; no doubt it was a way to stretch meat, albeit in a very tasty way. Cooking this way also preserved the meat, allowing it to be stored in the refrigerator over a period of time.

My brother, Paul Namkoong, came up with this recipe; I altered it a bit by changing the quantity of soy sauce and adding water to reduce the saltiness. I like to remove the cover of the saucepan for the last 20 minutes of cooking time so that the liquid reduces and becomes syrupy. The leftover sauce, flavored with the peppers, can be used to season other dishes.

Traditionally, brisket or shank cuts are used for this dish and the cooked meat is sliced thin to serve. We grew up eating chunks of changjorim, made with top round.

1½ pounds top round beef, cut into 1¼-inch cubes
1 green pepper, cored, seeds removed and cut into
  8 pieces
4 cloves garlic, coarsely chopped
2 fresh jalapeño peppers, seeds removed and cut into
  ½-inch pieces
⅓ cup soy sauce
1½ cups water
1 tablespoon sugar
1 tablespoon sesame oil

Combine all items in a shallow saucepan so that the meat is in one layer. Over medium high heat, bring the mixture to a boil, then reduce the heat and simmer, covered, for 1 hour. Uncover and continue too cook, checking for tenderness with a fork. Continue to cook until the meat is very tender and the liquid is slightly thickened. Remove from heat and cool. Store in a covered container in the refrigerator.

# Pulkogi
## Barbecued Beef Slices
*Serves 4*

P ulkogi, or fired meat, is a Korean classic, simply thin slices of beef, marinated and grilled. For this dish, beef is sliced thin, an eighth- to quarter-inch in thickness. Marinate the beef in Basic Korean Sauce for just an hour; if you marinate the beef too long, the salt from the soy sauce will break down the meat fiber and cause the beef to become mushy.

Rib eye is the traditional cut of beef used for this dish. Chuck is always a tasty cut; sirloin and eye of the round are also good. I sometimes marinate a New York steak, beef tenderloin or flank steak, without cutting, and cook it on the grill.

Pan frying and broiling are also options for pulkogi. This dish is often served with ssam—lettuce or perilla leaves—and rice.

**1 pound beef cut of choice**
**⅓ cup Basic Korean Sauce (page 66)**

Slice beef thin and place in a bowl. Pour sauce over and mix well. Cover and refrigerate for an hour.

When ready to cook, heat a charcoal or gas grill. Oil the grilling rack, using a paper towel soaked in oil. Over high heat, grill the pieces of meat for about 2 minutes on each side, until brown and crusty. Serve at once.

To broil, heat broiler and position oven rack about 4 inches from broiler unit. Using a baking pan lined with aluminum foil, arrange the slices of beef in one layer. Broil for 2 minutes on each side or to desired doneness.

To pan fry, heat a cast iron or other heavy skillet over high heat. Add oil to coat the skillet and when it is hot, add the pieces of beef in one layer. Cook for 2 minutes, turn and cook the other side. Transfer to a serving plate; spoon any pan juices over the meat.

*Meats & Seafood*

# Song Do Tchim
# Braised Meats and Vegetables
*Serves 12*

Hazel Pahk Chung grew up at 'Ewa Plantation, where her parents cooked for sugar plantation laborers. Her father was a minister and Hazel married Euicho Chung, minister of Korean Methodist Church. Her daughter Eldean Scott shared this recipe which was presented at a Hawaiian Electric Company program in May, 1987. "I remember pitting the dates, shelling the pine nuts and pounding the sesame seeds. This was not fun but this dish was yummy, spooned over rice, making it worth the work."

2 pounds boneless beef stew meat
2 pounds pork butt
2 pounds chicken
1 (8.5-ounce) can bamboo shoots
1 medium carrot, pared
1 large daikon, pared
3 stalks celery
4 green onions
1½ ounce red dates, soaked
1 (13.5-ounce) can chestnuts in heavy syrup
½ cup shelled pine nuts
3 cloves garlic, cut into halves
½ cup soy sauce
¼ cup sesame oil
3 tablespoons toasted and ground sesame seeds
2 tablespoons salt

Cut beef, pork and chicken into 2-inch pieces. Cut bamboo shoots, carrot, daikon, celery and green onions into 1-inch pieces. Remove seeds from dates; cut dates and chestnuts into halves.

Place all the ingredients into a large saucepan and cook on high heat for 10 minutes. Toss the mixture; lower the heat and simmer 15 more minutes. Toss again; cover and simmer for 1 hour.

# Taeji Pulkogi
# Spicy Barbecue Pork

*Serves 4*

This is a delicious, spicy dish that is best eaten with crunchy lettuce leaves and rice. Grill, cook under the broiler or pan fry the pork over high heat; cook the pork until well done and crisp on the edges.

For this recipe, use pork belly, cut into quarter-inch thick slices. Or use slices of pork shoulder (pork butt), cooking the steak-like pieces whole, then cutting them into bite-size pieces to serve. The fattiness of these two cuts is ideal for this dish; you can use pork loin if you want to cut down on the fat but it will not be as moist and delicious as pork belly or pork shoulder.

The recipe for this very tasty marinade is by Onjin Kim. This recipe makes about 1½ cups of marinade, enough for about 3 pounds of pork.

**1½ pound pork (see above)**

*Marinade:*
- 2 tablespoons rice wine
- 2 tablespoons soy sauce
- 4 tablespoons kochu jang (chili pepper paste)
- 1 tablespoon kochu karu (chili pepper powder)
- 2 tablepoons sugar
- 2 tablespoons corn syrup or honey
- 1 tablespoon grated ginger
- 1½ tablespoons minced garlic
- ¼ onion, minced
- 3 tablespoons chopped green onion
- 1 tablespoon sesame seed, roasted and ground
- 1 tablespoons sesame oil
- ½ teaspoon black pepper

Cut the pork into thin steaks or if you are using pork belly, into ¼-inch thick bite-size pieces.

*continued on page 76*

Combine all the other ingredients in a large bowl and mix together. Set aside half of the marinade in a covered jar, refrigerate and reserve for later use. Add the pork to the remaining marinade and mix well. Marinate for at least 2 hours in the refrigerator or overnight.

Heat a grill to medium high heat. Oil the grill rack, then place the pork on the grill. Cook the pork until well done.

If you are using a broiler, position rack about 6 inches from the broiler unit. Place the pork in a foil-lined pan in one layer. Broil for 2 minutes, turn the pieces and cook until well done.

Serve the pork with crisp lettuce leaves or grilled onions and rice.

---

# Tahkkui
# Korean Barbecue Chicken
*Serves 4*

*B*arbecue chicken is not a traditional Korean preparation; it's one of those "only in Hawai'i" dishes. Why not marinate chicken in a tasty sauce, then grill it at the beach? Chicken is as popular a protein as beef in Hawai'i so this dish has become a part of the Hawai'i Korean repertoire—it's not usually found in Korea or Korean cookbooks.

**8 to 10 pieces chicken, drums, thighs or wings**
**⅔ cup Basic Korean Sauce (page 66)**

Rinse chicken pieces in cool water and pat dry. Place in a pan and pour marinade over. Marinate for 4 to 6 hours, covered, in the refrigerator.

Remove chicken from refrigerator 30 minutes before cooking. Heat a grill and cook chicken over medium heat, turning frequently so it does not burn. Cook until well done.

Or, cook under a broiler, about 6 inches from broiler unit. Use a baking sheet lined with aluminum foil and place chicken pieces on foil. Broil for 5 to 7 minutes per side, turning pieces so they do not burn.

# 'Chicken Alice' Chicken Wings

### Serves 8

This is not a typical Korean dish but it epitomizes the bold Korean flavor that became very popular in Honolulu in the 1980s. Alice Yang invented this finger food in her Korea House Bar and served it in her restaurant, Chicken Alice. These establishments are gone now but the memory of this dish has lived on.

In this dish, Yang used Park's brand kimchi sauce, a bottled concoction of chilies and garlic, available in supermarkets throughout the state. Deep-frying makes the wings crunchy, a technique that is important to the success of the dish.

This recipe, obtained from Yang by Honolulu Star Advertiser *food writer* Betty Shimabukuro, *was printed in the* Honolulu Star Bulletin *in February 2005.*

**5 pounds chicken wings**
**Vegetable oil for deep-frying, Wesson brand preferred**
**⅓ cup Park's brand kimchi sauce**
**1 tablespoon minced garlic**
**2 tablespoons salt**
**2½ cups flour**
**2 cups water, or more, as needed**

Rinse and dry chicken. Cut off and discard wing tips. Cut through joint to separate drumettes from other half of wing.

To make batter: Combine kimchi sauce, garlic, salt and flour. Add water gradually, enough to make a thick batter, about the consistency of pancake batter.

Add chicken pieces to batter, mix well and marinate in refrigerator 2 to 3 hours.

Heat oil to 350°F. Deep fry chicken pieces about 10 minutes, until chicken rises to surface and coating is deep brown.

# Tahk Tchim
# Braised Chicken
*Serves 6*

**W**hat could be better than chicken braised in a Korean barbecue sauce? Add some vegetables for a delicious meal-in-a-pot to serve over rice.

**3 to 4 pounds whole chicken or chicken parts**
**⅔ cup Basic Korean Sauce (page 66)**
**10 dried shiitake mushrooms, soaked**
**2 medium white radish**
**2 large carrots**
**2 tablespoons salad oil**
**½ cup water**

Cut chicken into serving pieces and place in a bowl. Pour Korean Sauce over and let stand for 1 hour.

Remove stems from mushrooms; cut caps into halves. Peel and cut radishes and carrots into 1-inch pieces.

Drain chicken, reserving marinade. In a deep saucepan, heat the oil over medium high heat. Add the chicken, skin side down, and cook until brown and crusty on all sides. When all the chicken pieces have been browned, add the marinade, vegetables and water. Bring to a boil then cover, reduce the heat and simmer for 15 minutes. Remove the cover and continue to simmer until chicken and vegetables are cooked.

If you want a thicker sauce, mix 2 tablespoons of cornstarch with an equal amount of water. Remove the chicken and vegetables; add the cornstarch to the liquid in the pan and bring to a boil to thicken. Return chicken and vegetables to the pan and cook for another 5 minutes. Serve at once.

# Taegu
# Spicy Shredded Codfish

*Makes about 1½ cups*

The stinky smell of fish would emanate from the parish hall at Korean Christian Church after morning services every Sunday in the early 1960s. The halmuni, the older women of the church, would spend their Sunday afternoons shredding codfish that they prepared into taegu, selling it to raise money for the church.

This was the real and the best taegu, soft and chewy, perfectly seasoned and delicious, made from salted codfish. No one seems to make it this way anymore, perhaps for good reason because it requires hand shredding the codfish (not squid or other fish product) and putting up with the smell!

Dried, salted codfish is available in some supermarkets and at Korean supermarkets. A pound of dried, salted codfish will yield just over three-quarters of a pound of shredded meat. It's worth the effort!

**1 pound dried, salted codfish**
**3 tablespoons sesame oil**
**3 tablespoons honey**
**3 tablespoons roasted sesame seeds**
**2 tablespoons soy sauce**
**1 tablespoon kochu karu (chili pepper powder)**

Soak the codfish in water for several hours to remove the salt and soften the fish. Change the water every hour or so and taste the fish for saltiness. Continue to soak until the fish is pleasantly salty to your taste. Drain and pat dry. Remove skin and bones and break fish into small pieces. Shred the fish by hand into thin strips. Place in a bowl.

In a bowl, whisk together the remaining ingredients. Pour over the codfish and mix well. Let stand for an hour before serving.

# Seafood Stew

*Serves 6*

While assembling all the recipes I knew for this book, it occurred to me that we rarely ate seafood prepared in a Korean way when I was growing up. We ate fish—sashimi with cho kochu jang (page 117), fish chon (page 54), butterfish cooked with soy sauce and green onions, canned sardines with ssam (page 123). But clams, shrimp, crab, mussels, squid (except dried squid toasted over an open flame), and lobster—these were not part of my family's Korean repertoire, perhaps because few of these are found in Hawaiian waters and they were (and still are) expensive items.

But the Korean peninsula is surrounded by water and the bounty of seafood has a star role on the Korean table. One of the best ways to enjoy the variety of seafood is a stew, a Korean-style bouillabaisse. Onjin Kim demonstrated this recipe for a Hawaiian Electric Company cooking show in 1990.

12 shrimp
½ pound ʻōpakapaka fillet or other white fish
½ pound salmon fillet
½ cup white wine
¼ cup lemon juice
3 tablespoons kochu jang (chili pepper paste)
2 tablespoons soy sauce
3 tablespoons chopped green onion
4 teaspoons minced garlic
1 teaspoon minced ginger
¼ pound fresh shiitake mushrooms
2 tablespoons sesame oil
1 medium onion, sliced
Dash of salt
1½ cups water
12 steamer clams, rinsed
6 cooked crab claws
1 cup cilantro sprigs
2 tablespoons chopped fresh basil

Shell and clean shrimp. Cut opakapaka and salmon into 1-inch cubes.

In a bowl, combine wine, lemon juice, kochu jang, soy sauce, green onions, garlic and ginger. Add shrimp and fish; marinate for 1 hour. Drain marinade and reserve.

Remove stems from mushrooms and cut caps into quarters and set aside.

In a large saucepan, heat the sesame oil. Add the onion and sauté until transluscent. Add the mushrooms and salt; cook for 2 minutes. Add the reserved marinade and water. Cover and bring to a boil; cook for 10 minutes. Add the clams and marinated seafood; cook until calms open, about 1 minute. Add crab claws and cook until just heated. Serve in bowls; garnish with cilantro and basil.

# Spicy Sardines

*Serves 4 as a side dish*

*S*ardines, cooked with onions and kochu jang makes for a tasty bundle to wrap in a lettuce leaf with hot rice. It's so quick to make and it was a delicious staple food when I was growing up.

**2 cans sardines in oil**
**1 round onion, sliced thin**
**2 tablespoons kochu jang (chili pepper paste)**
**¼ cup water**

Drain the sardines, saving the oil. In a small skillet over medium heat, add a tablespoon of the oil. When it is hot, add the onion and sauté for a few minutes until translucent. Add the kochu jang and water and mix well. Add the sardines and break them up into bite-sized pieces. Reduce the heat and cook for 5 minutes to blend the flavors. Transfer to a serving bowl and serve with ssam (lettuce leaves) and hot steamed rice.

# Popcorn Shrimp

*Serves 6 as a side dish*

While perusing the aisles of Korean supermarkets in Honolulu, I came across a package of tiny, bright red, whole dried shrimp, about an inch in size with heads and tails. These light and crunchy shrimp are used, I am told, to enhance soup stocks. But I thought they would make a terrific popcorn-like appetizer. So I pan fried them with a little sesame oil, soy sauce, sugar and chili pepper; they're delicious to munch on and terrific on top of hot rice.

2 teaspoons sesame oil
1 cup small whole dried shrimp
1 tablespoon soy sauce
2 teaspoons sugar
½ teaspoon kochu karu (chili pepper powder)

In a frying pan that will hold the shrimp in a single layer, heat the sesame oil over medium heat. Add the shrimp and toss, coating the shrimp well. Add the soy sauce, sugar and kochu karu and continue to fry until the shrimp are crispy, dry and seasoned, about 10 to 15 minutes. Reduce the heat if necessary to prevent any burning. Remove from heat and cool; store in an airtight container until ready to serve.

# Korean-Style Poke

Poke (pronounced poh-kay) is Hawaiʻi's favorite dish, bite-sized morsels of seasoned fish or seafood, usually fresh ʻahi (tuna) from local waters. Fish markets and supermarkets offer a wide variety of prepared poke and there's always a "Korean-style" poke, usually seasoned with soy sauce, sesame and garlic.

Since ʻahi poke is really seasoned sashimi (raw fish), the quality of ʻahi is important. The ʻahi should be of good color, firm texture and be fresh. Two ways to make Korean-style poke:

## Poke I

**1 pound fresh ʻahi**
**3 to 4 tablespoons Basic Korean Sauce (page 66)**
**2 teaspoons kochu karu (chili pepper powder, optional)**

Cut ʻahi into ¾ inch dice and place in a bowl. Just before serving, add the sauce and chili pepper powder. Toss together and serve at once.

## Poke II

For this poke, use one of the spicy table sauces (pages 117-121). They are perfect for poke!

**1 pound fresh ʻahi**
**3 to 4 tablespoons table sauce (pages 117-121)**

Cut ʻahi into ¾-inch dice and place in a bowl. Just before serving, add the sauce and toss together. Serve at once.

# Taegu Tchim
# Braised Codfish

*Serves 4 as a side dish*

Helen Choy made this dish, among many others, for her family, using in-gredients available in island supermarkets. Bacalau, or salted codfish, was in good supply in Hawai'i because Portuguese plantation workers used it in their cooking. This dish was served alongside vegetables and rice, providing a bit of protein during a time when fish and meat were not plentiful or affordable.

**1 pound salted codfish**
**¾ cup soy sauce**
**¼ cup sugar**
**½ cup green onions cut into ¼-inch pieces**
**8 cloves grated garlic**
**4 green chili peppers, chopped**

Soak the codfish in water for several hours to remove as much salt as possible, changing the water 2 or 3 times. Remove the bones and skin; cut the codfish into 1 to 2-inch chunks.

Combine remaining ingredients in a bowl.

Heat a skillet and add a little vegetable oil over medium high heat. Fry the pieces of codfish until golden brown. Remove from skil-let and pour off excess oil. Add the sauce and bring to a boil; lower heat and add the codfish. Cover and simmer for about 2 hours, until sauce thickens.

# Namul
## Vegetable Dishes

In a Korean meal, several of these seasoned vegetable dishes would be served. In a Western context, namul might be considered a salad; generally, it is a terrific way to eat vegetables.

Any vegetable is a good candidate for making namul, raw or blanched. Seasonings vary from cook to cook; some use soy sauce in place of salt to season the vegetables. Some will add fresh chopped garlic. There are no rules except those dictated by your taste buds.

# Oi Namul
## Cucumber

*Serves 4 as a side dish*

1 large cucumber, preferably Japanese
2 teaspoons salt
1 tablespoon rice vinegar
1 teaspoon sugar
¼ teaspoon kochu karu (chili pepper powder)

Split cucumber in half lengthwise. With a spoon, scrape out the seeds. Cut cucumber into slices ⅛ inch thick and place in a bowl. Sprinkle with salt and mix together; let stand for at least an hour to draw out the water in the cucumber.

Rinse the cucumber and drain. Squeeze the cucumber to extract more water. Place in a bowl. Add the vinegar, sugar and kochu karu and mix together.

# Sigumchi Namul
## Spinach

*Serves 4 as a side dish*

1 pound spinach
2 tablespoons Cho Kochu Jang (page 117)
Roasted sesame seeds

Bring a large pot of water to a boil. Wash the spinach well and drain. When the water is boiling, add the spinach and cook for 1 minute, just enough to wilt the leaves. Drain in a colander and cool.

When the spinach is cool enough to handle, squeeze by the handful to extract the water. Place in a bowl. Add the Cho Kochu Jang and mix together well. Garnish with sesame seeds.

# Kaji Namul
## Eggplant
*Serves 4 as a side dish*

**2 Japanese eggplant**
**3 tablespoons Cho Kochu Jang (page 117)**
**Toasted sesame seeds for garnish**

Place eggplant in a steamer and steam until very soft. Cool.
Cut off the ends of the eggplant and with your hands, strip the eggplant into long pieces. Place in a bowl. Mix with the Cho Kochu Jang, adding more if needed. Sprinkle with sesame seeds and serve.

# Sukchu Namul
# Mung Bean Sprouts

*Serves 4 as a side dish*

1 (12-ounce) package mung bean sprouts
1 tablespoon sesame oil
¾ teaspoon salt
1 tablespoon roasted sesame seeds

Bring a large pot of water to a boil. Add the bean sprouts and cook for 1 minute, just enough to wilt the bean sprouts but maintain their crunchiness. Drain in a colander and rinse with cool water.

Squeeze the bean sprouts by the handful to extract water. Place in a bowl. Add the sesame oil, salt and sesame seeds and mix well.

# Kong Namul
# Soybean Sprouts

*Serves 4 as a side dish*

1 (8-ounce) package soybean sprouts
1 tablespoon oil
3 tablespoons Basic Korean Sauce (page 66)
2 green onions, chopped
1 tablespoons roasted sesame seeds

Clean the sprout heads and trim the ends of the sprouts. Rinse and drain.

In a saucepan, heat the oil over medium high heat. Add the soybean sprouts and stir-fry for 2 minutes. Add the sauce and cook another 2 minutes. Add the green onions and sesame seeds and mix well. Transfer to a serving dish and serve.

# Fresh Ogo, Cucumber and Crab Salad

*Makes 6 servings*

Ogo is the Japanese name for limu manauea, a red Hawaiian seaweed with stiff stems and branches. One of the most popular of edible seaweeds because of its mild succulence, slight saltiness and crunchiness, ogo is found at fish markets and supermarkets, the product of commercial farms rather than ocean harvesting. On Jin Kim created this dish for a Hawaiian Electric Company cooking demonstration in 1992.

½ pound fresh ogo (seaweed)
2 medium Japanese cucumbers
½ pound crab meat, shredded
3 tablespoons rice vinegar
3 tablespoons soy sauce
1 tablespoon sugar
2 teaspoons toasted and ground sesame seed
½ teaspoon kochu karu (chili pepper powder)
¼ teaspoon salt

Wash and blanch ogo; cut into 2-inch lengths. Pare and cut cucumbers in half lengthwise; thinly slice crosswise. In a large bowl, combine ogo, cucumbers and crab. To make the dressing, combine remaining ingredients. Just before serving, pour dressing over ogo mixture; mix well.

# Lettuce with Hot Chili Dressing

*Makes 6 servings*

This dish is all about using fresh, crisp lettuce and putting a Korean dressing on it. I'm not sure it's very traditional since Koreans don't really eat salads as such. But it's delicious and a great way to add a tasty salad to any meal. Romaine lettuce, especially baby romaine, is excellent in this preparation, its firm leaves and crunchy ribs providing good texture. But red leaf, butter or Mānoa lettuces are perfect too. The dressing is by chef On Jin Kim, who demonstrated this for Hawaiian Electric Company in 1990.

1 head red, butter or Mānoa lettuce
2 tablespoons soy sauce
2 tablespoons vinegar
2 tablespoons water
1 tablespoon sugar
1 teaspoon sesame oil
1 teaspoon crushed sesame seed
½ teaspoon kochu karu (chili pepper powder)

Wash and dry lettuce; tear into bite-size pieces and place in a bowl. Combine the remaining ingredients; mix well. Just before serving, pour dressing over lettuce; toss gently.

# Shrimp-Vegetable Salad
# with Pine Nut Dressing

*Serves 6*

Pine nuts are quite delicious and often used in Korean cooking. Grinding them releases their oily essence and adds to the deliciousness of this salad dressing. On Jin Kim prepared this for a Hawaiian Electric Company cooking demonstration in 1990.

½ **pound shrimp**
1 **medium carrot**
1 **medium cucumber**
1 **Japanese pear**
5 **romaine leaves**
½ **cup shelled pine nuts**
¼ **cup rice vinegar**
¼ **cup soy sauce**
¼ **cup water**
1 **tablespoon sugar**
2 **teaspoons dry mustard**

Cook, peel and cut shrimp in lengthwise halves. Pare and cut carrot, cucumber and pear into julienne strips. Shred lettuce; place in center of salad platter. Arrange shrimp, vegetables and fruit alternately around lettuce in a spoke pattern. Grind pine nuts in a blender. Add the vinegar, soy sauce, water, sugar and mustard; blend well. Serve with salad.

# Kosari
# Fresh Fern Shoots

*Serves 4 as a side dish*

Known as kosari, bracken fern shoots are widely referred to as warabi in Hawai'i. Similar to a fiddlehead fern, Hawaiians refer to this as hōʻiʻo or, on Maui, as pohole; different names for a delicious fresh food found in markets throughout the state. This recipe by Helen Choy was shared by her daughter, Melvia Kawashima.

½ **pound fresh fern shoots**
1 **tablespoon minced garlic**
¼ **cup sesame oil**
3 **tablespoons soy sauce**
3 **tablespoons sugar**
2 **tablespoons roasted and crushed sesame seeds**
½ **teaspoon black pepper**

Bring water to a boil in a large saucepan. Add the fern shoots and blanch for 2 minutes. Drain in a colander and rinse with cool water. Drain well and cut fern shoots into 2-inch pieces. Place in a bowl.

Whisk together the remaining ingredients and pour over the fern shoots. Mix and serve.

# The Popularity of Korean Food in Hawai'i

The savoriness of garlic and soy sauce, tempered by sweetness. A hint of sesame oil and the spicy kick of chili peppers. The Hawai'i palate loves bold flavors and Korean food fits right in.

The healthfulness of this vegetable-centric cuisine also has contributed to its popularity. What could be better for you than a host of small plates of vegetables, each seasoned a little differently, to eat with rice? Even better, rice with grains, like barley, millet, sorghum and beans, a combination increasingly popular among Koreans. Steaming, grilling, pan frying and braising use less fats. Fermented foods like kimchi are said to be good for the digestive system. And despite the renown of kalbi and pulkogi, meat is eaten in only small quantities.

In other cities, Korean food is mostly eaten by Korean people; in Hawai'i, all ethnic groups share in the delights of this cuisine.

## Hostess Bars

The Asian-style bar where hostesses kept men company was a concept that U.S. servicemen brought back from tours of duty. Starting in the late 1950s, hostess bars began to take hold in Honolulu, erroneously known as "Korean bars." Erroneous because not all these bars were Korean; Japanese and Southeast Asian immigrants also owned and staffed the bars, cabarets and restaurants.

In 1976, according to the *Honolulu Star Bulletin*, about 50 of these bars were among 500 liquor establishments on O'ahu. Post-World War II and Korean War brides and immigrants often found work in these establishments.

Respectability aside, these bars had one common denominator: food was served with the drinks. No doubt kimchi, kalbi, chon, tae-gu, fried mandu and various other Korean dishes encouraged more drinking with their savory and spicy qualities. Patrons acquired a taste for these foods and when they became available outside the context of the bar, they were familiar and could be enjoyed with family and friends.

## Korean Food Manufacturers

Kimchi was perhaps the first Korean food to become commercially available to the small pre-World War II Korean community. A conversation with Ruth Shon Kiehm revealed that her mother, Chum Sang Shon, was one of the first commercial kimchi makers in Hawai'i. In 1939 she tried selling kimchi at a grocery store on North King Street in the Pālama area. It was a big hit with Japanese, Chinese and Filipino residents and she would make a batch every week that was sold in bulk rather than bottled.

In the same decade Theresa So Chun Kim started a kimchi business that was to become Joe Kim's, named for her son. Hannah Liu founded Kohala Kimchi in Kapa'au on the Big Island in 1949, and Ya Mul Kim started Kea'au Kimchi on the Big Island at about the same time. Helen Halm started her namesake Halm's Kimchi in 1955. These four dominated the kimchi market for years, each with its own flavor profile and loyal following. Kohala and Halm's are now under the Halm's Enterprises umbrella along with Kewalo, Sweet Charley, Man Nani, A-1 and High Max (page 39).

Park's brand Korean Sauces was founded in the late 1950s by Duk Pong Park, who had come to Hawai'i as a 17-year-old picture bride. She sold vegetables at a stall at Kekaulike Market in Chinatown and began making kimchi with discarded vegetable trimmings. Soon, she was selling the fresh kimchi sauce mixture that she assembled by hand. Her biggest clients were cooks at hostess bars.

Park's was taken over by her son Bob Ko in 1972; he standardized his mother's recipes and packaging and developed other products, like kochu jang, Korean barbecue sauce, taegu and cho kochu jang. When Ko was looking for a buyer, he sought out Mike Irish (page 38). The Park's brand continues today, satisfying a loyal following of local Korean foodies.

The number of Korean food manufacturers in Hawai'i has grown along with the Korean population since the mid-1960s. Many companies produce kimchi, barbecue and table sauces, and other condiments that are easily found in supermarkets. Mandu wrappers are supplied by Chinese noodle manufacturers. Ttok, Korean rice cake, is made fresh in Honolulu by two companies, Hae Dong Sang Hoe and Ko Hyang Duk Jip, which distribute their products through Korean supermarkets.

## Korean Supermarkets

In the 1930s Hawai'i farmers supplied many of the vegetables that Koreans used: cabbage, won bok, chives, eggplant, green onions, lotus root, soybean and mung beans, spinach, sweet potato, radish, watercress, garlic, ginger, leeks, mugwort, peppers, persimmon and squash. Even rice was grown in Hawai'i.

A 1933 publication shows that common Japanese foods derived from soybeans, such as soy sauce, miso and tofu, were probably made by women in the plantation camps and sold to the Korean community. Seaweeds, somen noodles, Ajinomoto and sesame oil were available as well. Basic ingredients of soy sauce, miso, chili powder, garlic, ginger, green onions and sesame oil gradually became available in supermarkets, in demand by East Asians who settled here.

Then in the 1970s, markets that specialized in Korean products opened in Honolulu.

In 1976, Hyo Kyu Lim was contemplating his future as a student in agronomy at the University of Hawai'i at Mānoa. He decided to open a grocery with his wife, Hae Joo; Dae Han store on Kalākaua Avenue served the neighborhood with the usual assortment of soft drinks and groceries. Hae Joo began preparing a small selection of panchan, Korean side dishes, to sell in a small section of the store.

Word spread and customers, Korean and non-Korean, came for the kimchi and panchan and, as time went on, foods of the Korean pantry. Inventory was stored in the family's garage and the children helped in the store.

The family business expanded; in 1987 Pālama Market opened in Kapālama, then on Makaloa Street in 2004, and Waimalu in 2009. A new Kapālama location on King Street opened in 2013. The supermarket focuses on what Korean cooks want: fresh produce and select meat cuts, bottled and packaged sauces, noodles, seasonings and frozen foods. A wide array of kimchi and prepared foods is freshly made with a home-style quality, relished as comfort food. Today Pālama Market is the largest of the Korean food stores on Oʻahu.

Queen's Supermarket attained firm footing in 1999, when brothers Jason and Harrison Lee took over a near-bankrupt Korean market. Like Pālama Market it caters to Korean cooks and food lovers, as does the newer Keeaumoku Supermarket. All these markets have served to expand the availability of ingredients, Korean imports and ready-to-eat, freshly made Korean dishes, leading to a wider variety of dishes available in Honolulu.

## Korean Restaurants

These eateries brought the cuisine to the general public beginning with Korean Kitchen in 1950 and my father's Korean Garden in 1952. In 1970 Honolulu had about a dozen Korean restaurants; 40 years later there were about 60, according to telephone directories. Perhaps you remember some of these: Arirang, Kim Chee I, II, II, Camelia, Doraji, Frog House, House of Park, Koreana, Shon's, Sorabol, Willow Tree and Yu Chun.

These restaurants cater to local tastes. For one, they offer larger portions, especially at take-out, fast-food places where price and quantity equal value to the customer. This is very true of places like Yummy Korean Barbecue and its many offshoots. Korean sit-down restaurants, known for panchan or side dishes, serve a variety of kimchi and namul as part of the meal.

Korean food in Hawaiʻi is taking a turn, following trends in Korea toward lighter, healthier dishes that use less oil, sugar and salt. Restaurants in Korea have become specialized in specific dishes like vegetarian temple food, handmade noodles in soup, pork belly and fusion dishes. These trends are seen in the area referred to as Koreatown, centered on Keʻeaumoku Street. Some restaurants are offering a higher quality of ingredients, such as better grades of meat, sesame oil and soy sauce.

Still, on the Hawai'i Korean table, protein-based entrees, particularly beef, are the star, not just a side dish. Meat once was considered a luxury in a Korean home, prepared in small amounts and stretched to feed a family. Greater supply and affordability of beef, pork and chicken have given it a more prominent role.

Modern Korean chefs are fusing traditional items with Western ingredients and techniques. Pulkogi pizza is a tasty combination with seasoned beef and cheese atop a crispy rice crust. Ttok (rice cake), cut into bite-sized morsels, floats in a creamy cheese sauce spiked with chili peppers, imitating Italian gnocchi with a hint more chewiness. Pibimpap is served on a bed of bacon-kimchi fried rice. Hyoe doep pap is a popular dish of rice, greens and tuna sashimi with a spicy dressing, a mingling of American, Japanese and Korean food tastes.

Hawai'i chefs of all ethnic backgrounds and culinary training are using basic Korean flavors—soy sauce, sesame, garlic, chili pepper—in non-Korean dishes. One chef uses kimchi in a Reuben sandwich in place of sauerkraut. A salad dressing heavily flavored with kochu jang (Korean chili paste), is drizzled over salad greens or crisp fried calamari. Korean kalbi, braised with demi glace, is served with wasabi-flavored mashed potatoes.

## Korean Food as Fast Food

The first Patti's Chinese Kitchen opened at Ala Moana Center in 1967. It was a new concept in fast food—your choice of two, three or four dishes plus rice or noodles for very little money. It was also a new concept in the delivery of an ethnic cuisine, which had always been cooked to order and served family-style. Steam tables and warmers kept fresh-cooked batches of Chinese food hot and appetizing. A diner could have a varied selection of Chinese dishes on one plate. Patti's was very successful and spawned many similar establishments in a variety of cuisines.

Almost two decades later, the concept was applied to Korean food. Yummy's Korean Barbecue entered the fast-food scene with Korean barbecued beef and chicken, mandu, kuksu, soups and stews, all cooked to order while your pressed foam plate was filled with two scoops of rice and four vegetables chosen from among more than a dozen selections. Yummy's had a McDonald's quality to it: clean, brightly lit, well organized and efficient in delivering good, consistent food and value.

The brain behind Yummy's was Peter Kim, an immigrant from Korea who has called Hawai'i home since 1974, when he came to Hawai'i at age 15. After attending college in Alabama, Kim returned as his family was getting ready to open a restaurant. Kim pitched in and never left the business.

Kim capitalized on the local taste for Korean barbecued meat, which was becoming popular in Hawai'i in the 1980s, partly, he admits, because of hostess bars. In 1986, when he opened Yummy's, he recognized that he had to cater to the Hawai'i palate and its preference for bold, somewhat sweet barbecue and well-seasoned side dishes—unlike the more subtly seasoned traditional Korean foods. He added macaroni salad, a local favorite, potato salad and corn to his selections of kimchi and namul. Yummy offered customers a hefty plate of freshly prepared food at an affordable price.

"Fast casual" is the term Kim applies to his award-winning Yummy restaurants. He is modest about his role in popularizing Korean food, but there is little doubt that Yummy's spread Korean barbecue through the community.

## K-Dramas

KBFD, Hawai'i's Korean-language television channel, was pivotal in the K-drama phenomenon and had a positive influence on the Korean food scene. KBFD aired these "Korean soaps" and provided English subtitles, building a wide and loyal audience that has come to know Korean culture and food through entertainment.

Traditional Korean food culture was the theme of "Dae Jang Geum," the epic story of a woman who becomes the chief palace cook and later pharmacist, highlighting Joseon-era royal court cooking. "The Grand Chef" tells the story of a modern-day restaurant that features traditional cooking, and its intersection with contemporary food society. Both dramas interlace fabulous food scenes with food history and culture, and they are deliciously addicting.

KBFD also airs other K-dramas with food themes—*Bread, Love and Dreams, Delicious Proposal* and *My Name is Kim Sam-soon*— as well as cooking programs. The station's role in drawing attention to Korean food in Hawai'i is as prominent as the Food Network's in popularizing food and cooking nationwide.

## Japanese Influences

The Japanese occupied Korea for 35 years, ending in 1945, and there is no doubt that this influenced the cuisines of both nations. We can see a few examples, like the Korean inclusion of tamuji—the Korean word for takuan, the yellow pickled radish of Japan—within the repertoire of pickled vegetables prominent on the table. Kim pap, a roll of seaweed, rice and vegetables, meat and egg, is akin to Japanese futomaki. And was it okonomiyaki, the Japanese pancake, that gave rise to the pancakes of the Korean table, or was it the other way around?

Korean cooks routinely use Kikkoman soy sauce and Kadoya roasted sesame oil, two Japanese brands. Old-time Hawai'i Korean cooks still rely on Japanese miso, sweeter than its Korean counterpart, a product that was made in Hawai'i or imported from Japan before the time of Korean supermarkets.

One ingredient present in Korean food pre-1960s was monosodium glutamate, MSG. In old cookbooks and food articles, MSG was used in almost every dish to enhance its flavor and gain umami, or savoriness. This Japanese-discovered ingredient is still the subject of controversy as to its effects on individuals. Like salt, it is less prominent today in recipes and restaurant preparations.

## Only in Hawai'i

There are several idiosyncrasies about Korean food in Hawai'i, those "only in Hawai'i" things partly due, I think, to a culinary time warp. The first wave of immigrants (early 1900s) brought a cuisine limited in ingredients and preparations to what was available in Korea at the time. Succeeding generations stuck with what they knew. Count me in this group, familiar with a limited repertoire of ingredients and preparations, and expecting all Korean food to taste like my mother's.

Later immigrants, from the 1950s and especially post-1965, have brought a whole other dimension of Korean food to Hawai'i. The growth of the Korean economy enhanced food production and made available a wide assortment of ingredients. The refined dishes of palace cooking became popular as Koreans accessed this part of their past. This newer cuisine has made its way to Hawai'i, sometimes leaving old timers in a quandary as to what to order in a Korean restaurant.

A few dishes in the Hawai'i-Korean repertoire are unique to the state. Meat chon is one. In Hawai'i we marinate thin slices of beef in the traditional Korean marinade/barbecue sauce. Then we dip the slices in flour and egg and fry quickly to a golden brown. In Korea, meat chon is usually small pieces of beef, seasoned with salt and pepper, dipped in flour and egg and fried. Hawai'i's altogether different preparation is served as an entrée rather than a side dish.

Another Hawai'i-centric dish is Korean barbecue chicken. Few Korean cookbooks offer a recipe for chicken marinated and grilled like beef; chicken parts are uncommon in Korean supermarkets. Whole chickens or Cornish game hens are cooked in broth with ginseng as a medicinal dish, but marinated and grilled chicken is rare.

Local brands of kimchi (page 38) are generally different from the kimchi made by more recent immigrants. Generally, local brands are saltier, less chili-pepper red and have less fish or seafood flavoring. Today's kimchi looks deceptively spicy because of the kochu karu (powdered chili pepper) that is very red but often not very piquant. Fish, shrimp or oysters are often a part of the kimchi sauce, too.

## How sweet it is!

When you talk to old timers, descendants of the first Korean immigrants to Hawai'i, and ask "How has Korean food changed?" every person will say that the food has become sweeter. Many will wrinkle their noses as they say that, because the sweetness has become too pronounced.

Years ago I wrote an article for the *Honolulu Advertiser* about the making of kimchi by recent immigrants. I was startled to learn that their kimchi seasonings included sugar, an ingredient I had never used in kimchi. Even more telling is the sweetness of marinades for kalbi and pulkogi—that first bite of barbecued meat hits the sweet spot on your tongue.

Why has Korean food in Hawai'i become more sweet than savory? Many will say it is the influence of Japanese teriyaki. Certainly, Hawai'i's (and America's) penchant for sweetness has played a role in the evolution of Korean foods. Sauces, salad dressings, marinades, even Portuguese sausage have taken on a sugariness that sometimes overwhelms the savoriness of the dish. Could it be that we use more sugar because sugar was king as an agricultural crop in Hawai'i? Could it be that sweet carbonated beverages have accustomed our palates to sugariness?

Whatever the reason, restaurateurs routinely speak of adjusting their recipes to meet the sweeter palates of their local customers. Eating in Seoul is a different experience. The food is neither sweet nor salty; balance and subtlety in seasonings is the rule to the point that the food can sometimes seem bland. In Hawai'i, bold, pronounced flavors rule, making some popular Korean dishes truly unique to the islands.

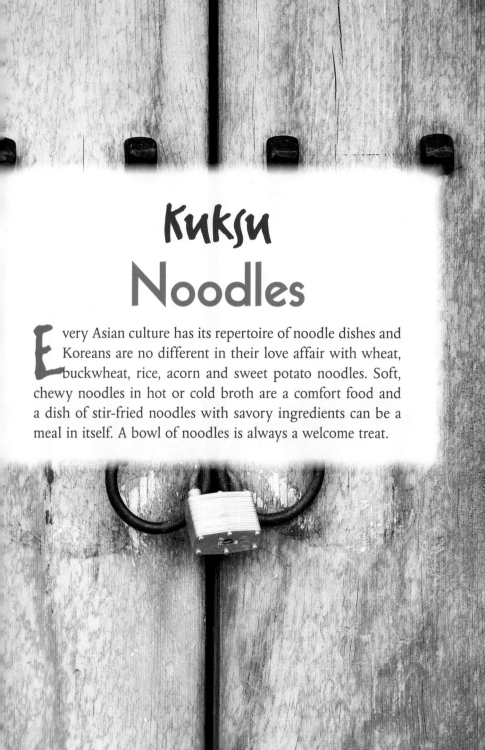

# Kuksu
# Noodles

Every Asian culture has its repertoire of noodle dishes and Koreans are no different in their love affair with wheat, buckwheat, rice, acorn and sweet potato noodles. Soft, chewy noodles in hot or cold broth are a comfort food and a dish of stir-fried noodles with savory ingredients can be a meal in itself. A bowl of noodles is always a welcome treat.

# Five Colors

Korean dishes and meals include an assortment of ingredients that reflect five colors: green, red, yellow, white and black. These colors are part of the five phases or cosmology of east Asia and are related to the five elements of wood, fire, water, metal and earth, respectively, and the tastes of sour, bitter, sweet, spicy and salty.

I did not grow up with this concept but learned it over the years. When planning a dish or a meal, I consider the colors of the ingredients and garnishes. Green might be green onions, cucumber or zucchini. For red I use chili peppers, carrots or red dates. Yellow and white are achieved by separating eggs and frying the yolks and whites separately into pancakes, then shredding the pancakes into thin strips or cutting them into diamond shapes. Black is provided by mushrooms and seaweed.

For garnishes, three colors are commonly used: yellow, white and green.

## Egg Garnish

In Korean cooking, an egg garnish is like parsley on an American plate—it's always there. To make it, you start with a pancake made of eggs. Separate eggs into whites and yolks. Beat each one well with a whisk or fork.

Heat a small skillet over medium heat and add a teaspoon or two of oil. Reduce the heat to low and pour in a small amount of egg white or yolks, swirling the pan to spread the egg into a thin pancake. Cook until the white is mostly set; do not brown. With a spatula, turn the pancake over and cook the other side. Transfer to a paper towel-lined plate.

When cool, stack the white and yellow pancakes separately and cut into fine shreds.

If you are following tradition, stews and soups are generally garnished with diamond-shaped white and yellow pieces. Cut the pancakes into ½-inch strips, then cut into diamonds.

# Chopchae
# Vegetables and Noodle Stir-Fry

*Serves 6 to 8*

Chopchae is Korean chop suey, a stir-fried mix of vegetables with clear noodles. Traditionally, each ingredient is cooked separately and cooled, then mixed together before serving at room temperature. But you can stir fry all the ingredients together, Chinese style, if you want.

Most of the old-time Korean cooks in Hawai'i use mung bean threads (also known as long rice, cellophane or glass noodles). But if you go to a Korean grocery store you discover that Korean cooks use sweet potato noodles, chewier than mung bean noodles and using a different cooking technique. Koreans are probably the only people that use sweet potato noodles!

Mung bean noodles are soaked, then cooked with a little liquid. Sweet potato noodles are not soaked at all; you put the brittle noodles into boiling water and cook them for 10 minutes. When they are cooked, they are drained, then added to your dish. After cooking, mung bean threads tend to be more slippery and softer than sweet potato noodles.

For chopchae, you can use an assortment of vegetables that you like and that are available. Besides the vegetables in this recipe, consider jicama (chop suey yam), bamboo shoots, won bok, watercress, bok choy, celery and bean sprouts. Also, fresh erynggi (alii) and tree ear (black fungus) mushrooms can be used. You can use as many as you like; you only need a small amount of each to make a sizeable dish. This recipe uses about 1 cup each of cut vegetables, a good amount to use per 1 ounce of noodles. I always err on the side of more vegetables in my chopchae. This also makes for an excellent vegetarian dish by omitting the meat; deep-fried tofu cut into strips would be excellent, too.

*continued on the next page*

4 ounces sweet potato noodles or mung bean thread
2 tablespoons oil
1 small round onion, thinly sliced
1 carrot, cut into 3-inch julienne strips
4 ounces beef or pork, cut into matchstick pieces
4 ounces green beans, cut into 3-inch julienne strips, about 1 cup
8 fresh or dried shiitake mushrooms, cut into thin strips
½ cup chicken broth or water
½ cup Basic Korean Sauce (page 66)
6 green onions, cut into 3-inch pieces and sliced thin lengthwise
Egg garnish (page 106)

For sweet potato noodles, bring a large pot of water to a boil. Break the noodles in half, add them to the boiling water and cook for 10 minutes. Drain and rinse with cool water. For mung bean threads, soak in water for at least an hour to soften. Drain and cut bundles in half.

Heat a wok or a large skillet over medium heat. Add the oil and when it is hot add the onion and cook until just soft. Add the carrot and cook for about 2 minutes. Increase the heat to medium high and add the beef and cook for about 1 minute. Add the green beans and mushrooms and stir-fry together. Add the noodles or bean threads and broth and cook for about 2 minutes. Add the Korean sauce and mix together. Add the green onions. Cook for another minute or two. Taste and adjust seasoning by adding more sauce if needed. Transfer to a serving dish and garnish with egg pancake.

# Naengmyun
## Noodles in Cold Broth
*Serves 4*

My mother made the best naengmyun ever, according to members of my family. Her naengmyun was not the kind you find in Korean restaurants today. She used somen noodles, rather than the traditional buckwheat or acorn noodles, and topped it simply with sliced pork, cucumber namul and hard-cooked egg slices.

It was the cold broth that made my mother's naengmyun delicious. It was, I believe, a combination of pork broth and kimchi juice. There was depth of flavor from the pork broth, acidity and spiciness from the kimchi juice. White radish kimchi juice is best but I sometimes use wonbok kimchi juice.

4 cups pork stock (page 159)
1 cup kimchi liquid, strained
Cooked sliced pork from making
  stock
1 (9-ounce) package somen noodles
Cucumber Namul (page 87)
2 hard-cooked eggs, halved or
  sliced
Ice cubes

Remove any fat that has solidified at the top of the pork stock. Mix the pork broth with the kimchi liquid; keep refrigerated.

Slice the pork into bite-sized pieces.

Bring a large pot of water to a boil. Add the somen and cook until done, about 3 to 4 minutes. Drain the noodles and rinse with cold water. Divide the noodles among 4 bowls. Top with slices of pork, Cucumber Namul and half an egg. Add a few ice cubes to each bowl. Ladle the cold broth over and serve.

# Píbimkuksu
## Sesame Noodles
### *Serves 3 as a main dish or 6 as a side dish*

*F*lavored with sesame oil and sesame seeds, this dish of noodles was a child-hood favorite. Simply prepared and served at room temperature, this noodle dish can stand on its own with some side dishes or it can be served as an accompaniment in almost any Asian-flavored meal.

**1 (9-ounce) package somen noodles**
**3 tablespoons sesame oil**
**1 tablespoon soy sauce**
**1 teaspoon kosher salt**
**¼ cup roasted and crushed sesame seeds**

Bring a large pot of water to a boil. Add the noodles and cook for 3 to 4 minutes. Drain the noodles in a colander and rinse with cool water. Drain well and transfer noodles to a serving bowl.

Drizzle the sesame oil over the noodles and mix well. Add the soy sauce, salt and sesame seeds and toss together. Serve at room temperature.

# Kuksu
## Noodles in Hot Broth
*Serves 4*

**A** steaming bowl of kuksu is as good as saimin or pho. I like to use flavorful homemade chicken broth which I make with stewing hens and keep in my freezer. When I'm ready to use it, I season it with salt or soy sauce; I like to keep it simple.

Somen noodles are my noodle of choice—it's the noodle I grew up on and there probably were no other kinds available until the 1960s onward. Somen is like Italian angel hair pasta: thin, tender, quick cooking and delicious.

**1 cup of shredded or sliced cooked chicken or beef from making stock (pages 157-158)**
**Sesame oil**
**6 cups chicken or beef broth, homemade (pages 157-158), or canned**
**1 (9-ounce) package somen noodles**
**Egg garnish (page 106)**
**2 green onions, cut into ¼-inch pieces**

Place the chicken or beef in a small bowl. Drizzle with a little sesame oil and sprinkle with salt to season. Set aside.

In a saucepan, bring the chicken broth to a boil. Season with salt or soy sauce to taste. Reduce heat to a simmer, cover and keep hot.

Bring a large pot of water to a boil. Add the somen and cook until done, about 3 to 4 minutes. Drain the noodles and divide among 4 bowls. Garnish with meat, egg and green onions. Ladle broth over and serve immediately.

# Panchan
# Side Dishes

Everyone who partakes of a Korean meal anticipates and relishes the little dishes of panchan or side dishes that include a variety of kimchi, namul, chon, tubu (tofu), kim, ssam and table sauces. All of these are to be eaten with rice, just a bite or two of panchan for each diner. Panchan offer a variety of flavors and textures to delight the taste buds alongside the "entrée" of meat, seafood or stew; the more panchan the merrier!

# Table Sauces

able sauces are essential to a Korean meal, adding zesty flavor and perhaps some heat to a dish. A table sauce can be as simple as kochu jang from the jar, a mix of kochu jang and toen jang, or any combination of ingredients and flavors that the cook can dream up. Here are 5 sauces, each different in its flavor profile, each packing some punch for whatever may be on the table.

## Cho Kochu Jang
## Spicy Table Sauce

*Makes about ½ cup*

*here are many, many Korean table sauces used to accompany chon, mandu, seafood pancakes and everything and anything else on the table. This is my version of a table sauce that I call cho kochu jang, a nice balance of spicy, sweet, sour and salty flavor components. Add more kochu jang if you want it hotter.*

2 tablespoons kochu jang (chili pepper paste)
2 tablespoons soy sauce
2 teaspoons sesame oil
2 tablespoons rice wine vinegar
1 tablespoon honey
1 tablespoon roasted sesame seeds

Measure all ingredients except sesame seeds into a bowl. Whisk together until well combined. Transfer to a serving dish and sprinkle sesame seeds over the top.

# Cho Kan Jang
# Mild Table Sauce

*T*his is a simple sauce for those who really don't want a spicy table sauce. It's a nice complement for fried foods like chon, balancing oiliness with a little acidity. I like to float thin slices of fresh red or green chili pepper in this sauce, adding color and just a touch of heat.

**2 tablespoons soy sauce**
**2 tablespoons rice wine vinegar**
**Fresh green or red chili pepper slices (optional)**

Mix the soy sauce and vinegar and top with chili pepper slices.

# Mustard Sauce
*Makes about ½ cup*

*I* like this sauce because it's a flavor departure from other table sauces that rely on soy sauce and chili pepper. Dry mustard is the predominant taste here and this is a good dipping sauce for raw fish, chon or kujeolpan.

**2 tablespoons soy sauce**
**4 teaspoons sugar**
**2 tablespoons rice vinegar**
**2 tablespoons water**
**4 teaspoons dry mustard**

In a small bowl, whisk all ingredients together.

# Kochu Jang
# Chili Pepper Paste

*Makes about 1 quart*

Kochu jang is the chili sauce of Korea, a thick, flavorful fermented paste used on its own or as an ingredient in many dishes. Unlike Southeast Asian chili sauces such as sambal oelek or Sriracha, which deliver straightforward chili pepper heat, kochu jang is a more mellow and full-bodied chili paste that can deliver different degrees of heat.

Kochu jang derives its flavor from fermented soybean paste (toen jang), rice and kochu karu (ground chili pepper).

While you can certainly buy this paste at a supermarket, it can be made at home. Agnes Rho Chun's recipe is simple and delicious!

**4 cups cooked rice**
**¾ cup white miso**
**⅔ cup honey**
**½ cup ground red pepper**
**3 tablespoons salt**
**2 tablespoons paprika**

Combine all ingredients in a large bowl and mix well. Pour into a 3 to 4-quart jar (the jar should be twice the volume of the mixture to allow for rising). Cover with foil or clear plastic wrap. Do not cover with jar lid. Let stand at room temperature for 1 month, until rice rises and becomes soft. (The mixture may be kept longer on the shelf without any harm. It will not mold. Do not refrigerate.)

Put 1 cup into blender, cover and blend until a soft paste is formed. Repeat until all is blended.

Put paste into a T-Fal or Teflon pan to prevent scorching. Cook over low heat, stirring frequently, until paste becomes thick and heavy with a glossy look; cool. Store in jar, covered with lid. Kochu jang does not need refrigeration.

# On Jin's Chili Paste Sauce

*Makes about 1 cup*

E very Korean cook has his or her version of *cho kochu jang*. Some will add minced green onion, some will add minced fresh garlic. Some will add both as Onjin Kim does in this recipe.

**5 tablespoons kochu jang (chili pepper paste)**
**5 tablespoons rice vinegar**
**3 tablespoons water**
**2 tablespoons sugar**
**1 tablespoon toasted and ground sesame seed**
**1 tablespoon chopped green onion**
**1 teaspoon chopped garlic**

Combine all ingredients.

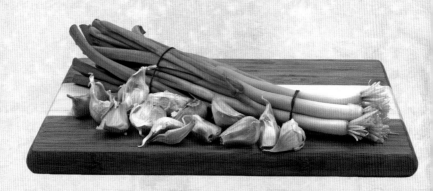

# Kelvin's Table Sauce

*Makes about ½ cup*

Kelvin Ro is one of my many chef friends and Korean, too! As the chef/ owner of Diamond Head Market and Grill, he serves kalbi plate lunches and other local-style dishes that are a cut above the usual plate lunch fare. This is his table sauce, a departure from the traditional Korean sauce, a fusion, if you will, of traditional flavors and contemporary ingredients and tastes.

¼ cup soy sauce
1 tablespoon kochu jang (chili pepper paste)
1 tablespoon rice vinegar
1 tablespoon sugar
1 teaspoon sesame oil
1 tablespoon ketchup
1 tablespoon chopped cilantro
1 tablespoon green onion
1 tablespoon roasted sesame seeds
2 tablespoons water

Whisk together all ingredients until well blended. Taste and adjust to personal taste. Let stand for at least an hour. Use with sashimi of fish and crab, mandu, chon, meats and other foods. Excellent for poke (seasoned bite-size morsels of raw tuna).

# Kim
# Toasted Seaweed

*Serves 4*

**K**im, toasted salted seaweed, is my all-time favorite Korean food. Crisp, salty and flavorful, kim (pronounced keem) is like potato chips and has become a favorite snack food for many. I can make a meal of kim and rice.

As a young girl, I remember preparing the kim: a folded sheet of seaweed was used as a brush to lightly oil each sheet of seaweed. A light sprinkle of salt from the salt shaker seasoned each piece. The stack of seaweed was rolled up into a log to await the toasting.

When it was time, my mother would heat a skillet and place a sheet into the pan. It would immediately shrink and crinkle, toasting to crisp perfection. She would stack the crisped sheets, then cut them into quarters, place them on a serving plate with each stack held in place with a toothpick.

I would watch carefully as my father deftly picked a piece of kim from a stack with his chopsticks, place it over the steaming rice on his plate and form a neat roll of kim and rice, the whole of which went into his mouth. It's a skill I have perfected today!

I still make kim the "old-fashioned" way, rejecting the prepared toasted seaweed found in markets everywhere ever since kim became a desirable snack food. The most difficult part of preparing kim is finding the very thin, lacy sheets of unprepared seaweed. Sushi nori is too thick; Korean supermarkets usually have one or two unseasoned varieties of thin seaweed. Freshly made kim is absolutely the best, incomparable to the convenience of packaged kim.

Plan on 2 to 3 sheets of seaweed per person as a side dish in a Korean supper. I use a blend of vegetable oil and sesame oil for the kim; sesame oil has a low smoke point and can burn easily so the mix of oils is ideal when toasting the sheets in a hot pan. The sesame oil, of course, adds great flavor.

**8 to 10 seaweed sheets**
**3 tablespoons vegetable oil**
**1 tablespoon sesame oil**
**Salt**

Lay the seaweed sheets on a flat surface. Blend the two oils in a small bowl. Using a pastry brush, lightly oil each sheet of seaweed. Sprinkle lightly with salt. Stack the sheets on a piece of waxed paper or plastic wrap.

When you have seasoned each sheet, roll the stack into a log and roll the waxed paper or plastic wrap around it. Let stand until ready to toast.

Heat a skillet on medium high. When it is very hot, place a sheet of seaweed into the skillet. Using chopsticks or tongs, quickly turn it over; it only takes a few seconds for the seaweed to shrink and crisp. Transfer the seaweed to a cutting board and repeat until all the sheets are toasted. Cut the sheets into quarters and transfer to a serving plate. Serve with rice.

# Ssam
# Lettuce Wrap

A staple of my childhood years was lettuce with rice and spicy sardines. I didn't know then what I know now: the lettuce wrap known as ssam is an important part of Korean cuisine and is used to wrap all kinds of foods including pulkogi, namul and whatever else is on the table.

Mānoa lettuce was always used for ssam but red or green leaf lettuce is also good. Baby romaine is a little crunchier and delicious for ssam; iceberg lettuce works, too. Sesame leaves and perilla leaves are used for ssam, too, as are thin slices of white radish and pieces of blanched won bok. Accompany ssam with a spicy table sauce, kochu jang, fresh sliced garlic and chili peppers.

# Muk I
# Mung Bean Jelly I

*Serves 4 as a side dish*

**M**uk is a dish I remember from my childhood that few old timers remember how to make. The thin white rectangular slices were pleasantly firm, somewhat bland except for their seasoning of sesame oil, salt and finely shredded dried seaweed; it was a deliciously refreshing dish. I remember my mother and friends trying to make this special preparation of ground mung beans, disconcerted when it didn't gel like it was supposed to.

Muk is another form of bean curd, the starchy essence of mung beans forming a firm Jello-like food. Today, most people make muk from mung bean powder, available at Korean supermarkets. Acorn jelly is also made from a packaged powder. Add water, cook, stir and pour into a mold. The mung bean muk is white, the acorn muk is brownish. Both can be served with vegetables and sauces, using the muk like it's a thick noodle.

Here's a recipe for mung bean muk made from scratch as best as I can put it together. I used the split mung beans; don't use the yellow split mung beans without their green shell because they include yellow food coloring and the muk will be yellow. This muk will be slightly green in color but much tastier than muk made from the powder.

**10 ounces (1½ cups) split mung beans**
**4 cups water**
**½ teaspoon salt**

Soak the mung beans in water for 4 hours. They will swell to about 3½ cups after soaking. Place half of the mung beans and water into a food processor or blender and purée until smooth. Pour the purée into a cheesecloth-lined strainer set over a 4-cup measuring cup or glass bowl. Gather the cheesecloth over the mixture and squeeze the liquid into the bowl. Repeat with the remaining mung beans.

*continued on page 126*

*Panchan*

Use the puréed beans to make Pindaettok (page 59) or discard.

After straining there will be about 3 cups of liquid. Let the liquid stand for 2 to 3 hours. You will notice layers form: foam at the top, brownish liquid, greenish liquid and white starchy liquid at the bottom.

After the starch has settled, scoop off the foam and brownish liquid; there will be about 1 cup of greenish liquid and starchy liquid left. Add water to make 3 cups of liquid total, about 2 cups. Mix well, incorporating the starch at the bottom.

Transfer the liquid to a saucepan and place over medium heat. Bring to a boil; the mixture will thicken quickly. Add the salt. Stir, lower the heat to a simmer and cook for 10 minutes, stirring constantly.

Transfer the mixture to a pan (an 8 x 8 inch pan works nicely) and cool. Cover and refrigerate until ready to serve.

To serve, cut the muk into 1 x 2 x ¼ inch pieces and place in a serving bowl. Drizzle with sesame oil and soy sauce; garnish with thin shreds of dried seaweed sheets. Or serve with a spicy table sauce.

# Muk II
# Mung Bean Jelly II

*Serves 4 as a side dish*

You can make mung bean muk using mung bean powder available at Korean supermarkets.

**½ cup mung bean powder**
**3½ cups water**
**½ teaspoon salt**

Bring 1½ cups of water to a boil in a saucepan. In a bowl, whisk together the powder and the remaining 2 cups of water. When the water is boiling, add the powder mixture and stir. Bring the mixture to a boil, stirring, then lower the heat to a simmer and cover. Cook for 20 minutes, stirring well every few minutes. The mixture will be thick and cloudy.

After 20 minutes, remove the cover and add the salt; mix well. Pour the mixture into a square pan and let cool. Cover with plastic wrap and refrigerate.

To serve, cut the muk into 1 x 2 x ¼ inch pieces and place in a serving bowl. Drizzle with sesame oil and soy sauce; garnish with thin shreds of dried seaweed sheets. Or serve with a spicy table sauce.

# Tubu Chorim
# Pan-Fried Bean Curd
*Serves 6 as a side dish*

**B**ean curd, tubu or tofu, is a staple of the Korean table and included in many a soup or stew. It is also eaten plain; I recall my mother serving fresh cold tofu topped with kimchi, a delicious combination with rice. I like to pan fry tofu and serve it with a table sauce, a simple dish that provides protein in a meal.

**1 block bean curd, about 20 ounces**
**Cornstarch (optional)**
**2 tablespoons oil**

Use medium to firm bean curd for pan-frying. Drain it well and slice a block into thick pieces, about 1-inch thick. Place the slices on paper towels and cover with a paper towel; press down gently to squeeze out more moisture.

You can coat the slices of bean curd in cornstarch before frying. This will make the exterior a little crisper but it's not necessary.

Using a skillet that will hold all the pieces in one layer, place it over medium high heat. Add the oil. When the oil is hot, add the bean curd slices. Cook the slices without moving them until the edges turn golden brown, about 3 to 5 minutes. You want a nice crust to form before you move the pieces, otherwise the crispy part will stick to your pan and the slice will break apart.

When the bean curd piece is nicely browned, turn it and continue to cook until the other side is golden brown.

When it is nicely browned, transfer it to a serving plate. Serve with a table sauce (pages 117-121).

Or, when the slices are brown, drizzle the pieces with 3 to 4 tablespoons Basic Korean Sauce (page 66). Cover and cook for 5 minutes; serve. This version will not be crisp but it will be quite tasty!

# Special Dishes

Special dishes have always marked celebratory occasions on the Korean calendar in Hawaii with the New Year perhaps the most celebrated of all. Ttok Kuk and Mandu are traditional, accompanied by an array of panchan. A few home cooks might attempt a Shinsollo or Kujeolpan, two dishes from the esteemed repertoire of Royal Court Cooking in Korea. And a special punch to cap off a Korean meal will surely delight!

# Mandu • Dumplings

Mandu are the equivalent of Chinese won ton and gau gee. Served in a flavorful beef or chicken broth garnished with vegetables, stir-fried strips of beef or chicken, green onions and egg, mandu is a meal in itself.

I always make mandu for the New Year celebration, serving it on top of ttok or rice cakes, the traditional good luck food. Panchan, meat, rice and kimchi are also part of the New Year's menu, a Korean feast for a worthy celebration.

Mandu is not a dish you make for just a few people—you make a lot of them for a crowd or freeze some for a future meal. The following recipe makes about six dozen, enough for eight hearty appetites.

You can make your own mandu wrappers but I choose to buy them from the Chinese noodle factories in Honolulu. Mandu wrappers are round rather than square and slightly thicker than won ton wrappers. Too thick a wrapper and you can't get enough filling into the dumpling; potsticker wrappers seem ideal. If your wrappers are too thick, roll them out with a rolling pin and cut with a biscuit cutter.

Shaping mandu takes a little practice, something you learn as you watch your mother do it. The round circle of dough is moistened on the edges with a beaten egg (I prefer egg to water; it "glues" the edges better), using your finger as a brush. A spoonful of filling is placed on one half of the circle, then the dough is folded in half and the edges pressed together well. Moisten the edge of the half circle with your finger dipped in egg. Then pinch the edges, five or six times, for the classic mandu look.

Mandu can be served in hot broth or simply boiled in water. You can also fry it crisp in lots of oil or steam-fry it like potstickers. A table sauce is always good for dipping.

There are many variations on the filling. The classic combination of vegetable (bean sprouts and/or cabbage), tofu and meat (beef, pork or a combination) is still my favorite, but other versions include long rice, kimchi, chicken, cilantro and watercress.

When making filling, always remember that you want to remove the water from vegetables and tofu, otherwise the filling will weep and weaken your wrapper, causing it break while cooking. But there still has to be enough moisture to keep the filling tender and moist. So squeeze the liquid out, but not all of it.

When seasoning the filling, err on the side of saltiness. When the filling is wrapped and the mandu cooked in boiling water, excess saltiness will dissipate.

# Mandu I
# Korean Dumplings I

*Makes 60 to 70 mandu*

*T*his is the combination of ingredients I use. It is pork based; many of my family members use beef or a combination of the two. It is the version of mandu I grew up with and love.

1 (20-ounce) block tofu
1 pound ground pork
3 teaspoons salt
1 (10-ounce) package bean sprouts
1 small head won bok, about 1 pound
4 green onions, finely chopped
2 tablespoons sesame oil
2 eggs, beaten in separate bowls
Mandu wrappers, about 60 to 70 pieces

Drain the tofu and place it in a cheesecloth-lined colander. Place a weight on top of the tofu to squeeze out the water. Let stand for about 30 minutes and allow tofu to drain.

Heat a large skillet and when it is hot, add the ground pork. Cook the pork, breaking it up into very small pieces. When the pork is cooked, season with 1 teaspoon of salt; mix well. Transfer the pork to a large mixing bowl and set aside to cool.

Bring a large pot of water to a boil. Add the won bok to the boiling water and blanch for 2 to 3 minutes or until wilted. With tongs, remove the won bok from the water and drain in a colander; rinse with cool water and drain.

In the same pot of boiling water, add the bean sprouts and blanch for 3 minutes. Drain the bean sprouts in a colander; rinse with cool water and drain.

When the won bok is cool, stack the pieces and cut crosswise into fine shreds. Coarsely chop the beansprouts.

Squeeze liquid from the tofu by gathering the cheesecloth around it and twisting it. Add the crumbled tofu to the mixing bowl with the pork, scraping bits from the cheesecloth.

Use the cheesecloth to squeeze out the water from the won bok and bean sprouts, adding each to the mixing bowl after the water is removed. Add green onion, sesame oil, 1 egg and remaining 2 teaspoons of salt; mix well. Taste the mixture and add more salt if needed.

To make the dumplings, moisten the edge of a wrapper with the remaining beaten egg. Place a spoonful of filling on half of the wrapper; fold the wrapper in half and seal the edges well. Moisten the edge of the half circle of wrapper and pinch the edge 5 or 6 times for a decorative edge. Place on a parchment-lined baking sheet and continue to make more dumplings.

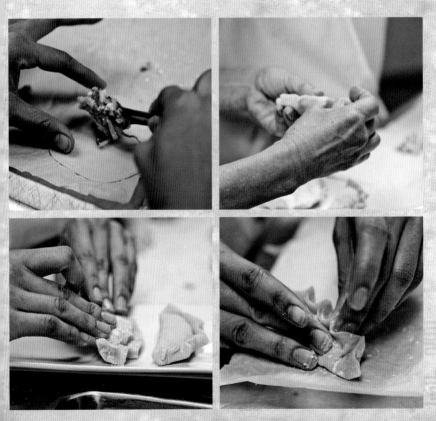

*continued on the next page*

If you're making the mandu ahead of time, you can refrigerate it for a few hours, covered with plastic wrap. You can freeze mandu for longer storage: Place in the freezer on a baking sheet; when frozen place in a freezer storage bag and seal.

### To serve mandu:
Chicken or beef broth, about 1 cup per serving
¼ teaspoon sesame oil per cup of broth
Salt to taste

### Garnishes:
Egg garnish (page 106)
Green onions, cut into ¼-inch slices
Seaweed, toasted and crumbled into pieces
Beef or chicken garnish (page 141)
Sil kochu

### Table Sauces (pages 117-121)

Heat broth in a large saucepan until boiling. Add sesame oil and salt to taste. Reduce heat, cover and keep very hot.

To cook the mandu, bring a large pot of water to a boil. Drop mandu into the boiling water, being careful not to add too many at a time. If you are cooking frozen mandu, add them to the boiling water directly from the freezer. Cook the mandu for 3 to 4 minutes; when they float to the top, cook for another minute before removing them with a slotted spoon or strainer. Drain well and transfer to individual serving bowls, about 6 to 8 per serving as a main dish. Garnish as desired. Ladle boiling broth over the mandu. Serve with egg garnish and green onions and any other garnishes you are using. Serve at once with table sauce.

# Mandu II
# Korean Dumplings II
*Makes 60 to 70 mandu*

**H**elen Choy made large tubs full of filling to be shaped into dumplings and served on New Year's Eve for dozens of guests. Melvia Kawashima, her daughter, remembers spooning filling into the mandu wrappers and pinching the edges closed. "There were six to eight trays of mandu covered with damp cotton dishtowels to keep the wrappers from drying out. A large stockpot of brewing beef bones for the stock was on the stove. Mom was an amazing one-woman catering event."

Helen Choy's recipe includes long rice and cilantro, a combination used by other old-time Hawai'i Korean cooks. The long rice replaces the soft texture of tofu and cilantro adds a different flavor dimension. Cilantro is not a traditional Korean ingredient; it is just becoming available in Seoul markets.

**2 ounces mung bean threads (long rice)**
**1 (16-ounce) package bean sprouts**
**1 small head cabbage**
**¾ pound finely ground pork**
**1 pound finely ground beef**
**½ cup minced green onions**
**2 tablespoons minced garlic**
**2 to 3 tablespoons minced cilantro**
**2 teaspoons salt**
**1 teaspoon black pepper**
**60 to 70 mandu wrappers**

Soak the mung bean threads for 5 minutes.

Bring a large pot of water to a boil. Add the bean sprouts and cook for 2 to 3 minutes until limp. Scoop out the bean sprouts and place in a colander. Rinse with cool water and drain well.

Remove the core from the head cabbage and separate the leaves. In the same pot of water, cook the cabbage for a few minutes un-

*Special Dishes*

til limp. Scoop out of the water and place in a colander. Rinse with cool water and drain well.

In the same pot of water, cook the mung bean threads over low heat until tender. Transfer to a colander and drain well.

Chop the bean sprouts and cabbage—they should be chopped to small bits but not too fine. Using a piece of cheesecloth or your hands, squeeze out as much liquid as possible from the chopped vegetables. Place vegetables in a large bowl.

Chop the mung bean threads coarsely; add to vegetables in bowl.

Add the pork, beef, green onions, garlic, cilantro, salt and pepper to the bowl and mix together well. Cook a little of the mixture to taste for seasoning and adjust seasoning.

Fill and shape mandu wrappers as above.

# Kujeolpan
# Nine Ingredient Appetizer

Kujeolpan was a dish that intrigued me for years, the pretty arrangement of seasoned ingredients surrounding a stack of pancakes in a covered nine-sectioned lacquered box. No doubt this was a dish that came from Korean Royal Court cuisine; it is a visually beautiful dish, requiring some fine knife skills and time to prepare. Someone gifted me the box and this dish has become a unique and quite spectacular appetizer for special occasions.

The pancake used to wrap the ingredients is traditionally made with flour and water, one by one. I prefer to use a French crepe recipe for my pancakes, a richer and tastier pancake that always gets compliments. I like to trim them with a large round cutter before placing them in the center compartment.

The nine ingredients should, I believe, reflect five colors: eggs, separated for yellow and white; beef and mushrooms for black; vegetables for green; carrots for red. According to the many recipes I have seen, the vegetables can vary: mung bean sprouts, watercress, zucchini, spinach, cucumber, red and green bell pepper, green onions, leeks, bamboo shoots and white radish.

Oysters, abalone, clam, fish, shrimp, red dates and pine nuts can also be included in the selections. Each is cut into matchsticks or thin shreds, cooked and seasoned separately. The diner selects a bit of each ingredient and places it in a pancake. A table sauce accompanies the filled pancake.

continued on the next page

# Pancakes I

Traditional pancakes for Kujeolpan are made with equal portions of flour and water and a pinch of salt. The ingredients are whisked together and the pancakes are cooked in a small, well-oiled skillet over medium heat.

# Pancakes II

**1 cup flour**
**3 eggs**
**1 tablespoon melted butter**
**½ teaspoon salt**
**1⅓ cups milk**
**Vegetable oil for cooking**

Place first five ingredients in a food processor or blender and mix together until smooth. Let stand for an hour.

Use a small skillet or crepe pan. Heat the pan over medium high and brush with oil. Ladle about 2 tablespoons of batter into the pan and swirl the batter to form a thin pancake, about 4 inches in diameter. Cook until light brown. Flip pancake and cook the other side. Transfer to a plate. Continue to make pancakes until all the batter is used.

Using a round metal cutter, cut the pancakes into rounds that will fit into the center of the kujeolpan tray. Makes about 30 pancakes, approximately 3½ inches each.

# Eggs

In two small bowls, separate 2 eggs. Beat the whites and yolks separately.

Heat a small skillet over medium low heat and add a little cooking oil. Pour ⅓ of the whites into the hot pan and swirl the pan to form a thin pancake. Turn to cook other side; cook until whites are set but do not brown. Transfer to a plate. Repeat until all the whites are cooked, adding more oil if needed. Cook the yolks in the same way.

Stack the whites and roll into a log. Slice into thin shreds and place in kujeolpan tray. Do the same for the yolks.

# Carrots

Cut one carrot into fine matchstick pieces, about 2 x ⅛ inches. Heat a small skillet and add 1 teaspoon of oil. Add the carrots and sauté briefly; add 2 teaspoons Basic Korean Sauce (page 66) to season. Cook for 1 minute. Transfer to kujeolpan tray.

# Mushrooms

Cut fresh or dried, soaked mushrooms into 2 x ⅛ inch strips; about ½ cup. Heat a small skillet and add 1 teaspoon of oil. Add the mushrooms and sauté briefly; add 2 teaspoons Basic Korean Sauce to season. Cook for 1 minute. Transfer to kujeolpan tray.

# Beef or Chicken

Cut beef or chicken into 2 x ⅛ inch strips, about ½ cup. Heat a small skillet and add 1 teaspoon of oil. Add the meat and sauté briefly; add 2 teaspoons Basic Korean Sauce to season. Cook for 1 minute. Transfer to kujeolpan tray.

# Vegetables

Use 3 vegetables from the list on page 139. Cook each separately in a small skillet, seasoning each with soy sauce and sesame oil or with a little Basic Korean Sauce. Cook for 1 minute; vegetables should retain a little crunchiness. Transfer each to kujeolpan tray.

Fill each compartment of the kujeolpan tray with a prepared ingredient. Pancakes go into the center. Serve kujeolpan at room temperature with table sauces on the side.

# Sujunggwa
# Persimmon and Cinnamon Punch
*Serves 6*

his is a delightful "tea" flavored with ginger and cinnamon. It's the perfect ending to a Korean meal, sweet and refreshing. I learned to make this at a cooking class in Seoul; the instructor told me it was important to simmer the ginger and cinnamon separately.

**6 cups water**
**1 ounce fresh ginger, peeled and sliced thin**
**1 (4-inch) cinnamon stick**
**½ cup sugar**
**2 dried persimmons**
**1 tablespoon pine nuts**

Divide water into two saucepans. Add ginger slices to one pan, cinnamon sticks to the other. Place each pan over a burner and bring to a boil; simmer for 30 minutes. Strain the liquid into one container, discarding the ginger and cinnamon sticks. Add the sugar to the liquid and stir to dissolve. Cool and refrigerate.

Open the dried persimmons so they are flat; remove any seeds. Slice the persimmon into thin strips. Place a few strips into a small serving bowl or teacup and add the chilled liquid. Sprinkle with a few pine nuts and serve.

**Variation:** Another garnish for this refreshing drink is to roll the dried persimmon around a whole shelled walnut, pressing it so that the walnut is encased in the persimmon. Slice the roll and place the slices in a small serving bowl or teacup. Add the chilled liquid and serve.

# Shinsollo
# Korean Hot Pot
*Serves 4 generously*

This is a dish representative of palace cooking in Korea. My great grand-mother was a seamstress in the Yi Dynasty royal court and no doubt learned a few cooking techniques and recipes during her time there. Presumably she passed this on to my grandmother Elizabeth Pahk Choi who prepared this dish for a Pan Pacific Union dinner in November 1931.

As a young adult in the 1970s, I urged my mother to make shinsollo, which she did for a Honolulu Advertiser *article in December 1972. It was really the only time she made it, but it was impressive. One of these days I'll make it, too.*

### Marinade:
¼ cup soy sauce
2 cloves garlic, minced
Slice fresh ginger
2 green onions, chopped
2 tablespoons sesame oil or vegetable oil

½ pound sirloin, thinly sliced
½ pound ground beef
½ pound mahimahi
½ pound calves liver
Salt
Oil for pan-frying
¼ cup gingko nuts
1 medium-sized white radish
1 teaspoon sugar
Flour for dredging
2 eggs
6 eggs, separated
6 large black mushrooms, soaked in water

*continued on the next page*

1 bunch watercress
12 Chinese red dates, soaked and sliced
½ cup blanched walnuts
⅓ cup pine nuts
2 cups rich chicken broth
4 to 6 green onions, cut into 2-inch pieces

Mix marinade ingredients and divide in half in two bowls. Marinate sirloin and ground beef separately in each bowl for 15 minutes.

Lightly sprinkle mahimahi and liver with salt.

In a small skillet, heat a teaspoon of oil. Saute gingko nuts until green. Remove from pan, cool and peel. Set aside.

Bring a medium saucepan of water to boil. Peel radish and slice into thin bite-sized pieces. Add sugar to water then add radish; cook for 3 to 5 minutes or until just tender. Drain and cool; set aside.

Place flour in a shallow bowl or pan. Beat the 2 eggs in a shallow bowl. Heat a skillet over medium high heat. Dip sirloin pieces in flour then coat in egg. Add a tablespoon of oil to the skillet and fry the sirloin pieces until golden brown on one side. Flip and fry the other side. Transfer to a paper towel-lined plate.

Form small ¾-inch balls with the ground beef. Dip in flour and egg and fry in oil, turning and browning all sides. Transfer to a paper towel-lined plate.

Clean the skillet. Repeat the dipping and frying with the mahimahi and liver. When the meat, fish and liver are cool, slice into 2 inch by ½-inch wide strips. Set aside.

Clean the skillet and heat over medium heat. Add a tablespoon of oil. Beat the egg whites and yolks separately in bowls. Make a thin pancake of the egg whites over medium low heat; do not brown. Transfer to a plate. Repeat with the egg yolks. When the egg pancakes are cool, slice each into 2 x ½ inch wide strips, keeping them separate. Set aside.

Slice the mushrooms into thin strips and set aside. Cut watercress into 2-inch pieces and set aside.

Just before serving time, have pieces of lit charcoal ready; they should fit into the center chimney of the shinsollo pot.

Have all the ingredients ready to assemble in shinsollo pot. Ingredients will be arranged in two layers; use half of each item in each layer. At the bottom place the radish and watercress. Arrange the beef, meat balls, mahimahi and liver slices on top. Place the egg whites and yolks in the

*My mother making shinsollo.*
*(December 31, 1972—Star-Bulletin & Advertiser)*

next layer. Between the slices, arrange pieces of mushrooms, dates, walnuts, pine nuts and gingko nuts. Repeat the layer. At the top, arrange the green onions like spokes from the center.

Heat the chicken broth. Season with salt to taste. Bring to a boil. Pour the boiling broth into the shinsollo pot to the top of the ingredients. Place charcoal in the center. Cover pot and let the dish cook until onions are wilted. The shinsollo is ready to serve.

Serve shinsollo by carefully spooning food onto plates or small bowls. Shinsollo may be served with rice or whatever else is desired.

Appendix

# The Korean Pantry

The Korean pantry is a simple one; most Hawai'i home cooks already have the key seasonings—soy sauce, garlic, ginger, green onions, chili peppers, sesame oil and seeds. With meats, poultry, seafood and fresh vegetables, cooking a Korean meal is undoubtedly uncomplicated.

Korean supermarkets and Asian grocery stores have made specialty ingredients more accessible. Actually, I do not recognize many items in the Korean supermarkets, as I did not grow up with them. But these items lead to delicious adventures.

## Bean (Kong)

Yellow and black soybeans, mung beans, adzuki beans, and red and black kidney beans are often cooked with rice and other grains to provide more nourishment. Mung beans are ground into a flour and cooked with water to make Muk, a kind of "jelly" served with seasonings (page 127). Ground mung beans also make Pindaettok, a tasty fried chon (page 59).

## Chestnut (Pam)

Fresh chestnuts, available in the fall, are delicious boiled or roasted. Their sweet flavor and soft texture are delicious in a variety of sweet and savory dishes. They are essential to Yak Pap, the sweet medicinal rice (page 18), and are included in Kalbi Tchim (page 69). If you cannot find fresh, look for frozen, peeled and ready to cook. Dried chestnuts are soaked for several hours to reconstitute. Canned chestnuts, drained of syrup, can also be substituted for fresh.

## Chili pepper (Kochu)

Fresh red and green chilies add flavor, heat and an important visual note as a garnish. Straight, smooth three-inch-long peppers such as serranos and jalapenos are the norm; small Hawaiian chilies and Thai bird chilies offer lots more heat. Fresh chilies do not store well in the refrigerator; I keep them in the freezer.

## Chili pepper powder (Kochu Karu)

Finely ground, coarsely ground or crushed dried chili pepper brings flavor, sweetness and heat. It is essential to that uniquely Korean red color of kimchi, stews and sauces. Not all these powders are fiery hot; some register more like paprika, mild and sweet. Choose and use powder according to your taste buds.

## Chili pepper thread (Sil Kochu)

One of the great finds in a Korean supermarket is a package of shredded dried chili peppers, bright red threads that can garnish a dish with great color, texture and just a bit of heat. Sprinkle a large pinch over a green onion or chive pancake, top off a bowl of steaming soup or include it in a stir-fry or sauté of any ethnic cuisine.

## Garlic (Manul)

If there is one herb that characterizes Korean food, it is garlic, the essential flavor in so many dishes. This "stinking rose" is a member of the lily family; its pungency and aroma are stronger than its cousins—onions, leeks, chives, green onions and shallots. Garlic's intensity also varies according to the variety you use.

Always use fresh garlic in Korean cooking. Buy whole bulbs that are heavy for their size, with smooth skins and few individual cloves. Store in a cool, dry place at room temperature, never in the refrigerator. Smash a clove with a knife blade to release the skin for peeling. Always remove the bitter green sprout in the center.

Raw garlic is sometimes used, but to mellow the flavor, cook it; always on medium- to medium-low heat to avoid burning and bitterness.

A medium garlic clove will yield about 1 teaspoon of minced garlic.

# Ginger (Saenggang)

This underground rhizome that is grown in Hawai'i offers a pungent, medicinal flavor when mature. Not as pronounced in Korean cooking as garlic, ginger plays a secondary though important role in seasoning.

Peel ginger if it is to be eaten as part of a dish; if it is to be removed before serving, as in a soup or stew, it may be left unpeeled. Peel with a knife or scrape the skin off with a spoon. To obtain ginger juice, grate or mince it fine, then squeeze the juice through a piece of cheesecloth. Ginger graters also work well to extract juice and leave the fiber behind.

Ginger can be stored at room temperature. A slice the size of a quarter will yield about 1 teaspoon of minced ginger.

# Onion (Yangpa)

Varieties used in Korean cooking include leeks, scallions (the common green onion), chives, garlic and shallots. Pa, the common green onion, is most ubiquitous, adding mild flavor and a sparkling garnish to many dishes.

## Noodles (Kuksu)

For old-time Koreans in Hawai'i, kuksu means somen noodles, the thin white Japanese wheat-flour noodles that have always been on market shelves. Chewy buckwheat, potato starch, acorn and other wheat noodles served in newer restaurants are different, but thoroughly enjoyable. Hot kuksu in a flavorful broth or cold kuksu (naeng myun) are staples. Potato starch noodles are used in Chopchae, light, colorless and flavor-absorbent. Buckwheat and acorn noodles are often served in cold soups; wheat noodles can be served in hot or cold broths.

## Mushroom (Posot)

Enoki, shiitake, wood ear and button mushrooms can be used in many dishes. Stone-ear mushrooms, usually dried, are used as a garnish, especially for ceremonial dishes, providing a jet-black color.

## Pine nut (Chat)

These seeds from pine cones lend their distinctive flavor to savory and sweet preparations. They contain a fair amount of oil and should be stored in the refrigerator or freezer to keep them from spoiling. Toasting pine nuts in a skillet enhances flavor. To add flavor but reduce oil, place pine nuts in a folded paper towel and chop them through the towel. The oil will be released as you chop and absorbed by the paper.

## Radish (Mu)

Koreans do not use the typical red radish that Westerners use for garnishes or salads. It is daikon, or giant white radish, that is pickled as kimchi, or used in soups, stews or side dishes. Some of these radishes are denser in texture, others smaller with pony tails of green attached. Tamuji, yellow pickled

*The Korean Pantry*

radish (takuan), figures prominently in Kim Pap (Korean sushi), both an influence of Japanese cuisine. Radish is often referred to as turnip, but these are two different vegetables.

# Red date (Taechu)

Also known as jujubes or Chinese red dates, these are not the same as the palm dates of the Middle East or North Africa. Jujubes are cultivated in China and India, and are valued for their medicinal qualities in Korean cuisine. Rarely available fresh, dried jujubes need to be soaked in water; they are used in sweet and savory preparations.

# Rice (Ssal)

Medium grain, sticky rice is preferred, steamed to perfection and served at every meal. Cooked rice is referred to as pap.

# Rice cake (Ttok)

Korean rice cakes are firmer and denser than their Japanese counterpart, mochi. Shaped into sticks or logs, rice cakes are sliced on the diagonal, softened in boiling water and served in soups (ttok kuk), savory stir fry dishes or grilled with meats. Thinner sticks are simmered in a spicy sauce for Ttok Boki, a popular street food in Korea.

A number of steamed ttok confections are served at celebrations: Silu Ttok (layered ttok with beans), Song Pyun (steamed half-moon cakes with sweet filling), Chal Ttok (rice cake with red beans). Plain discs of ttok, the texture of mochi, can be pan-fried until crisp and golden, then served with honey.

## Salt (Sogum)

Coarse sea salt is used to make kimchi and sauces, and for salting seafood and vegetables. Refined salt, similar to kosher, is used to season dishes. "Hawaiian salt" is often used in the islands for kimchi.

## Seaweed (Kim)

Different seaweeds figure prominently in Korean cooking. One is miyok, also known as wakame, a greenish-black seaweed used in soup or prepared for a salad. Thicker sheets of dried sea kelp (Japanese kombu) are used to add flavor to stocks or prepared for salads.

Laver, seaweed sheets or nori, is toasted and seasoned with sesame oil and salt to be eaten with rice, a preparation referred to as kim. Laver is also used to make Kim Pap, the Korean sushi roll. Note that Korean laver tends to be thinner and more delicate than Japanese sushi laver.

## Sesame oil (Chan Kirum)

Sesame oil, dark and aromatic, derived from roasted seeds, is a key flavoring in Korean food, more prominently employed than in other Asian cuisines. Its flavor is distinctive but also fleeting, so it is best to use it just before serving. It is not good for cooking as it has a low burning point. Always look for 100 percent sesame oil rather than a blend; Kadoya is a good brand.

## Sesame seeds (Kkae)

Sesame seeds are toasted to a light brown, then crushed to release their flavor, adding a prominent note in many dishes. The seeds are also important as a garnish.

Wild sesame (tulkkae), or perilla seed, is prominent in Korean cooking today, roasted, crushed and used like sesame seed as a seasoning. The oil from these seeds is also used for pan frying

## Soybean paste (Toen Jang)

Fermented soybean paste, known as miso in Japan, can be sweet to salty, mild to robust, smooth to chunky. It flavors soups and stews, marinades and salad dressings. Toen jang from Korea is usually more intensely flavored than the Hawaiʻi-produced Japanese misos that old-timers have used for decades because there was little else. Today, Korean and Japanese brands are abundant and their flavors and aromas vary widely.

## Soy sauce (Kan Jang)

This is the basic "salt" of Korean cooking, made from naturally fermented soybeans, wheat, yeast and salt. It was invented by the Chinese but perfected by the Japanese, who developed a natural brewing and fermentation process that yields a mellow and savory sauce.

Soy sauces, commonly known in Hawaiʻi as shoyu, differ in saltiness; Kikkoman is regarded as dense and salty; Yamasa is thinner, often preferred for fish. Both are naturally brewed and aged, giving them more depth and nuance. Kikkoman is the accepted brand for Korean cooking despite the many Korean brands available at Korean supermarkets. I often dilute soy sauce with a little water and sugar to offset the saltiness. There is no right or wrong soy sauce to use soy sauce—your taste buds will help you adjust the saltiness as needed.

Korean cooks also use kuk kan jang, or soup soy sauce, a clear sauce with a good amount of saltiness, to season a soup well.

## Soybean curd (Tubu)

Soybean curd, or tofu, is used in soups, stews and braised dishes; it is also pan-fried or deep-fried to be served with sauce. Silky, soft, firm and very firm varieties are used in different ways. Fresh soybean curd is available in all supermarkets; store it in a covered container and change the water frequently to keep it fresh.

## Sprouts

Two sprouts figure prominently on the Korean table. Mung bean sprouts (sukju namul) are the budlike, greenish, headed sprouts also known simply as bean sprouts. These are used in mandu filling, soups and stews or simply blanched and seasoned. Soybean sprouts (kong namul) are fatter, with large yellow heads, and are firmer in texture. Tails on soybean sprouts should be removed before they are used.

## Sweet rice (Chapssal)

Glutinous rice, or mochi rice, is steamed for confections or used in a savory stuffing. Sweet rice flour (chapsalgaru) is used in rice cakes, pancakes, and porridges; kimchi and kochu jang often include this rice as well.

## Vinegar (Shikcho)

For acidity and sourness, rice vinegar is preferred. Malt, sweet potato, apple, onion, brown rice and persimmon vinegars also figure in Korean dishes.

## Won bok (Paechu)

This pale, white- to light-green leafed cabbage is used mostly for making kimchi, the spicy pickled national dish of Korea. Won bok is also known as Napa or celery cabbage.

# Toasting Sesame Seeds

When I was a child, it was my job to pound the sesame seeds that my mother carefully toasted in a dry frying pan. They were nicely browned, then transferred to an old coffee tin. I would sit on a low stool in the garage, coffee tin on the ground, and crush the seeds using the butt of a hammer wrapped in foil. There was great pleasure in this task: the smell of warm sesame seeds releasing their aroma was intoxicating.

Greater pleasure came when the job was done: a little of the warm sesame seeds and a sprinkling of salt over a bowl of rice was delicious!

To toast sesame seeds: Place a half-cup of white sesame seeds in a small skillet over medium- to medium-low heat. Continuously shake the pan as the seeds will change from white to golden to golden-brown quickly. Keep a watchful eye. You'll hear the seeds pop as they toast and they may fly about. As soon as all the seeds are evenly toasted, remove them from the heat (they will darken a little more) and transfer to a mortar. Using a pestle, grind them to release their flavor. Toast and crush sesame seeds as you need them; the aroma and flavor are best when freshly prepared.

If you can find one, a spice toaster is ideal for toasting sesame seeds. It is a small round mesh basket with a lid and handle; you use it over the stove top, shaking it as seeds or spices toast.

# Stocks

Stocks are fundamental to all cuisines, adding flavor and depth to soups, stews and sauces. Western cuisines use beef, chicken, veal, fish and seafood; in the East it is much the same, with pork and seaweed also used as the basis for stocks.

## Anchovy Stock

*Makes about 3 cups*

Dried shrimp and fish stocks add savoriness to dishes. Here's Onjin Kim's simple anchovy stock that can be used with seafood-based soups and stews or in Ttok Boki (page 14). Dried anchovies, just an inch or two long, can be found in Korean supermarkets along with the sheets of thick dried sea kelp.

**20 pieces dried anchovy**
**6 ounces white radish**
**2 pieces dried sea kelp (kombu)**
**4 cups water**

Place all ingredients in a pot over high heat. Bring to boil, reduce heat to low and simmer 20 minutes. Pour through fine strainer; discard solids.

# Chicken Stock

*hicken stock is always a part of my pantry, usually homemade and in my freezer. It is used as the soup base for mandu, kuksu (noodles), kong namul kuk (soybean sprout soup) and other dishes that make a terrific meal in a bowl.*

*Make stock with a whole fryer or a stewing chicken, if you can find one. Backs, wings, necks and feet can be used on their own, or added to a whole chicken; the more bones you have the more flavor you can extract.*

**3 to 4 pound whole chicken or chicken wings, backs, necks and feet**
**Water to cover, about 12 cups**
**2 slices fresh ginger (optional)**

Place chicken in an 8- to 10-quart stockpot and cover with water by a few inches. Place over high heat and bring to a boil. Scum (proteins) will rise to the surface; skim so that your stock remains clear. When the liquid is boiling, reduce the heat so the liquid simmers and bubbles gently. Simmer at least 2 hours. Remove a piece of bone and taste the meat—when there's no flavor left, the stock is ready.

If you're using a whole fryer, cut it into quarters and after 30 to 40 minutes of cooking, remove the pieces and debone. Return the bones to the pot and save the meat for any other use.

Turn off heat. Using tongs or a slotted spoon, remove bones and discard. Let the stock cool a little before pouring it into another container through a fine strainer to remove any small bones and pieces of meat. Cool and refrigerate, covered, overnight. The next day, use a spoon to remove and discard the layer of fat that will solidify on top. Your stock is now ready to use or freeze in smaller containers. Makes about 8 cups.

For a more robust stock, place the strained stock over medium high heat and gently boil. As the liquid in the pot reduces through evaporation, the flavor will be more concentrated. Keep cooking until

*continued on the next page*

stock is half its original volume. Cool and refrigerate or freeze.

For an even more flavorful stock, use the stock to cook another chicken or batch of bones, simmering for a couple of hours. Strain and refrigerate or freeze.

# Beef Stock

*Makes about 8 cups*

In addition to bones, meat trimmings and a variety of cuts—eye of round, brisket, shanks, oxtails, flank, ribs, even tenderloin—are used in Korean beef stock, boiled until tender, and strained. This stock is easy and quick, requiring little time to achieve lots of flavor; the stock can be served as a soup with additional ingredients. The cooked beef is used to top noodles and other dishes.

For a richer, darker beef stock, roast the shanks or any bones you are using in a 375-degree oven until nicely browned. This is the traditional French way of making stock—roasting first, then extracting the flavor.

**4 pounds beef, with some bones**
**12 cups water**

Soak beef in water 30 minutes and drain. Place in 8- to 10-quart stockpot. Cover with 12 cups water and bring to boil over high heat. Remove any scum that rises to the top. Reduce heat so the liquid simmers and bubbles gently. Simmer about 1 hour.

Remove from heat and remove meat. The meat can be cut and served in the soup or stored for another dish. The stock should be strained, cooled and refrigerated, then and skimmed of any fat before using.

# Pork Stock

*Makes about 8 cups*

**P**ork stock is not common in Western cooking, but it is delicious as a base for soups and noodle dishes in Eastern cooking. Pork stock is the basis for my version of Naengmyun, cold noodles in broth (page 111), and a terrific addition to stews like Kimchi Tchigae (page 31) and Piji (page 34).

**3-pound piece of pork shoulder (pork butt) with bone**
**3 slices ginger**
**12 cups water**

Cut pork into 4 or 6 pieces and place in a 6- to 8-quart saucepan. Add ginger. Add water and bring to boil over high heat. Skim any scum that rises to the surface. Reduce heat so liquid simmers and gently bubbles. Simmer 2 hours or until pork is tender when pierced with a fork.

Remove pork from liquid and set aside to cool; cover and refrigerate. Pour liquid through a fine strainer. Cool and refrigerate. When ready to use, skim off the congealed fat.

The boiled pork can be sliced and served at room temperature with a table sauce or used as a topping for noodle dishes, hot or cold.

# Cooking Equipment

Korean cooking requires little special equipment. Pots and pans of cast iron, stainless steel with aluminum or other cookware of good quality and weight can be used for frying, braising and the making of soups and stews. Non-stick surfaces are popular but unnecessary. A wide skillet or frying pan and a wide, deep saucepan are probably the handiest pieces to have.

A good, sharp knife with a thin 8-inch blade is essential. Good cutting technique—slicing and julienne cutting—is a hallmark of a good Korean cook.

A grill, small or large, is ideal for meat dishes such as kalbi and pulkogi, enhancing the flavors. A steamer is nice for special rice dishes and sweets.

# Bibliography

Berlitz. *Korean Compact Dictionary*. New York, Berlitz Publishing, 2011.

Chang, Sun-Young. *A Korean Mother's Cooking Notes*. Seoul, Korea, Ewha Womans University Press, 1997.

Cho, Joong Ok. *Home Style Korean Cooking in Pictures*. Tokyo, Japan. Shufunotomo Co. Ltd. 1981.

Choe, Ji Sook and Moriyama, Yukiko. *Korean Cooking for Everyone*. Tokyo, Japan, JOIE, 1986.

Choo, Dave. "Deep Kim Chee." *Hana Hou Magazine*, Vol 14, No. 2.

Chu, Woul Young. *Traditional Korean Cuisine*. Los Angeles, California. The Korea Times L.A., 1985.

Chun, Injoo. *Authentic Recipes from Korea*. Singapore. Periplus Editions, Ltd. 2004.

Chung, Taekyung and Debra Samuels. *The Korean Table*. Vermont, Tuttle Publishing, 2008.

Corum, Ann Kondo. *Ethnic Foods of Hawai'i*. Honolulu, Hawai'i. The Bess Press, 1983.

Cost, Bruce. *Asian Ingredients*. New York, William Morrow and Company, 1988.

Choe, Yong-Ho, Ilpyong J. Kim and Moo-Young Han. *Annotated Chronology of the Korean Immigration to the United States: 1882 to 1952*. http://www.duke.edu/~myhan/kaf0501.html

Crawford, David Livingston. *Hawai'i's Crop Parade: A Review of Useful Products Derived from the Soil in the Hawaiian Islands, Past and Present*. Honolulu, Hawai'i, Advertiser Publishing Co. Ltd., 1937.

Han, Chung Hea. *Traditional Korean Cooking*. Seoul, Korea. Chung Woo Publishing Co. 1986.

Han, Stephanie. Salome Choi Han: *A Korean Woman in Hawai'i*. Research paper, 2000.

Hawaiian Electric Company recipe booklets: 1976, 1978, 1979, 1982, 1983, 1985, 1990, 1992.

Heckathorn, John. *Korean Restaurants in Hawai'i*. Honolulu Magazine, Nov. 2010.

Hepinstall, Hi Soo Shin. *Growing Up in a Korean Kitchen*. Berkeley, California, Ten Speed Press, 2001.

Hilts, J.D. and Kim, Minkyoung. *Korean Phrasebook*. Victoria, Australia, Lonely Planet Publications, 2002.

Hyun, Judy. *The Korean Cookbook, Quick and Easy Recipes*. Elizabeth, New Jersey. Hollym International Corp. 1970.

Jones, B. J. and Rhie, Gene S. *NTC's Compact Korean and English Dictionary*. Chicago, Illinois, NTC Publishing Group, 1995.

Kirkendall, Judith Midgely. *Hawaiian Ethnogastronomy: The Development of a Pidgin-Creole Cuisine*. PhD dissertation, University of Hawai'i, 1985.

Korea Foundation. *Traditional Food: A Taste of Korean Life*. Seoul, Korea, Seoul Selection 2010.

Kwak, Jenny. *Dok Suni*. New York, St. Martin's Press, 1998.

Laudan, Rachel. *The Food of Paradise*. Honolulu, Hawai'i, University of Hawai'i Press, 1996.

Lee, Chun Ja, Hye Won Park and Kwi Young Kim. *The Book of Kim Chi*. Seoul, Korea, Korea Information Service, 1998.

Lee, Florence C. and Helen C. Lee. *Kimchi: A Korean Health Food*. Elizabeth, New Jersey, Hollym Corporation, 1988.

Miller, Carey D. "Japanese Foods Commonly Used in Hawai'i." *Hawai'i Agricultural Experiment Station Bulletin* #68, Nov. 1933.

Millon, Marc and Kim. *Flavours of Korea*. London, Andre Deutsch Limited, 1991.

Morris, Harriett. *The Art of Korean Cooking*. Tokyo, Japan, Charles E. Tuttle Company Inc., 1959.

Namkoong, Joan. *Go Home, Cook Rice*. Honolulu, Namkoong Publishing, 2001.

Noh, Chin-hwa. *Traditional Korean Cooking: Snacks and Basic Side Dishes*. Elizabeth, New Jersey. Hollym Corporation, 1985.

Park, Allisa, ed. *Discovering Korean Cuisine: Recipes from the Best Korean Restaurants in Los Angeles*. Lomita, California. Dream Character Inc., 2007.

Patterson, Wayne. *The Ilse: First Generation Korean Immigrants in Hawai'i 1903-1973*. Honolulu, Hawai'i, University of Hawai'i and Center for Korean Studies, University of Hawai'i, 2000.

Pettid, Michael J. *Korean Cuisine: An Illustrated History*. London, Reaktion Books Ltd. 1008.

Yamaguchi, Roy. *Hawai'i Cooks*. Berkeley, California, Ten Speed Press, 2003.

Young, Jin Song. *Taste of Korea*. London. Anness Publishing Ltd., 2010.

*Honolulu Advertiser*

Today's Pitch, Oct. 3, 1953.
Korean woman toiled in camps, Jan. 7, 1973.
From laborer to leader in 70 years in Hawai'i, Jan. 11, 1973.
Koreans find help at Kalihi Pālama Center, Nov. 28, 1973.
Waking up from the American dream, May 26, 1974.
Kimchee Dynasty Matriarch, Aug. 22, 1977.
Classic Korean recipes, updated, Jan. 18, 1978.

Festive Korean dishes, May 13, 1987.
Now it's "lite" kim chee, Aug. 2, 1989.
She's cooking up a storm Korean style, Sept. 5, 1990.
A taste of Korean cuisine, July 22, 1992.
Bibimbap: A taste of Korean home cooking. Jan. 15, 2003.
Helen Halm, founder of Halm's Kim Chee, dead at 85. Dec. 2, 2003.
Koreans in Hawai'i: 100 Years of Dreams, Accomplishments; A Chronicle of the
    Last 100 Years. January 2003.
Noh Foods of Hawai'i a family affair, July 4, 2007.
Patti's Chinese Kitchen may revive, March 8, 2010.

*Honolulu Star-Bulletin*

Korean cook and shinsillo, Nov. 12, 1931.
Koreans will dedicate church on Sunday, Apr. 23, 1938.
Korean restaurant opens doors today, July 26, 1952.
Kimchee, teriyaki from a package, Dec. 21, 1966.
The kim chee begins with a package, June 9, 1971.
An angel pot dish stars for New Year's, Dec. 31, 1972.
Yung Ja Shin Story, March 25, 1973.
The hostess bar: an expanding business, Feb. 26, 1976.
A legacy of courage and hope, Jan. 12, 1978.
Short ribs, Korean-style, May 13, 1981.
A family who knows its sauces, Mar. 16, 1983.
Little Kapa'au factory packs a pickled punch, May 8, 1989.
If you like it hot, head for Willow Tree, Jan. 14, 1994.
Good fortune awaits patrons of Frog House, Mar. 4, 1994.
Chicken Alice, Feb. 16, 2005.

# Index

# About the Author

Joan Namkoong was born and raised in Hawai'i, where her father had a Korean restaurant in the early 1950s. She has been part of the culinary scene in the state since the mid-1970s, as the co-founder of The Compleat Kitchen retail stores and then as the food editor of the *Honolulu Advertiser*. As a freelance food writer, author and consultant, she has written numerous articles and books and has been involved in establishing farmers markets in Hawai'i.

---

The photographs for this book were taken at Leeward Community College with the enthusiastic assistance of students from an Asian/continental cuisine class at LCC. The students tested the recipes and prepared each dish for its moment in the spotlight. Many thanks to chef-instructor David Millen, whose efficiency and wealth of knowledge kept us on track each day.

# Other Best-Selling

## Star ★ Advertiser

## Cookbooks

168 pp. • 6 x 9 in.
softcover

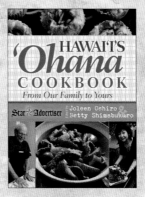

216 pp. • 6 x 9 in.
softcover

176 pp. • 6 x 9 in.
softcover

240 pp. • 9 x 9 in. • hardcover

224 pp. • 9 x 9 in. • hardcover